# The Luckiest Girl
## in the world

# The Luckiest Girl
## in the world

**Verity Sweeny Purdy**

**Foreword by Betty Oliphant**

**Heritage House**

Copyright © 1998   Verity Sweeny Purdy

CANADIAN CATALOGUING IN PUBLICATION DATA

Purdy, Verity Sweeny, 1922-
The luckiest girl in the world

ISBN 1-895811-57-0

1.  Purdy, Verity, 1922-
2.  Dancers—Biography.
I.  Title.

GV1785.P87A3   1998      792.8'028'092      C98-910124-X

First Edition  1998

Heritage House wishes to acknowledge Heritage Canada, the British Columbia Arts Council, the Ministry of Small Business, Tourism and Culture, and Canada Council for supporting its publishing program.

Cover & book design: Catherine Mack, Cairn Consulting
Front cover photo: Fred Arundt

HERITAGE HOUSE PUBLISHING COMPANY LTD.
Unit #8 - 17921 55th Ave., Surrey, BC V3S 6C4

Printed in Canada

# Acknowledgements

I owe a debt of gratitude to Audrey Grescoe whose enthusiasm got me started on this project one summer in France, and to Betty C. Keller whose patience, wisdom and encouragement kept me writing. I am in awe of my editors, Audrey McClellan and Betty C. Keller, without whose painstaking and caring guidance I would have been well out of my depth.

I am also deeply indebted to the following relatives for the use of photographs from their own histories to illustrate this book;

Andrew Bell-Irving, who with his family now lives at Bankside, for pictures of Shum, her house, and hunting in Dumfriesshire.

Maureen Owen, now living in Australia, for pictures of Thirlestane Castle, Makerstoun, Djan and J.J. Bell-Irving, Olly, the twins and herself.

John Robb of London who photographed Cheyne Cottage as it is today.

Patricia (Trish) Wilson of Vancouver for pictures of The Strands and Grandfather Bell-Irving.

Roger Sweeny of Vancouver for pictures of Grandfather Sweeny, Ben, Bimbo and Doffie.

# CONTENTS

# FOREWORD

I find it incredibly moving that I have been asked to write the foreword for Verity Purdy's book as her life story parallels mine in so many ways. Like me, she dedicated herself to dance at an early age. The very nature of a career in dance demands, while we are still children, an independence and a capacity for self-discipline that would not ordinarily be expected until we were approaching adulthood.

Eleven-year-old Verity left her home in Vancouver in order to get the best dance training which at that time was in London, England, where I lived. As I read about her life there, I relived many of my own experiences: the wonderful performances at Drury Lane, Covent Garden and Sadler's Wells; the superb actors and dancers who inspired us and gave meaning to our choice of a profession on stage; the pageantry of the funeral of King George V and the coronation of his son, George VI.

The similarities extended to our family lives. I also had aristocratic, sometimes snobbish relatives in Scotland. My sister lived on Cheyne Walk in Chelsea, close to where Verity lived for some time with her crippled Aunt Doffie who had suffered as a child with tubercular spine. My daughter also suffered from this ailment but her body, thanks to modern medicine, was not nearly as badly distorted as Doffie's was.

I also knew many of the leading teachers with whom Verity studied. In fact, one of them, Sheilagh Elliott-Clarke, and I were to become fellow examiners of the Stage Branch of the Imperial Society of Teachers of Dancing.

I did not meet Verity until 1949, just a short time before she left Toronto with her husband for New York. She asked me to take over her senior students which I did with pleasure as they were superbly trained. And now I feel I have come to really know her through her book.

Verity's dreams and determination to succeed gave her the courage to face the many difficulties in her training and she overcame them with amazing maturity. It could not have been easy but, as the title of her book tells us, she considers herself to be *The Luckiest Girl in the World.*

Betty Oliphant, C.C., LL.D., D.Litt.,
and Governor General's Award winner.
*Toronto, July 1997*

# THE LUCKIEST GIRL
## IN THE WORLD

Bewildered, I stood like a clown in the midst of my first London dancing class. No other child had bulgy bloomers or knobby knees like mine. Their bloomers were discreetly hidden beneath their neat little tunics, their knees were straight and their toes pointed out. What's more, they all knew exactly what Miss Bedells expected them to do.

I looked up to see my crooked-backed Aunty Doffie glaring at me from her chair by the window. It was her money that would pay for my dance training. She must be able to see—as everyone in the room—that I would never make a dancer.

I wanted to cry but I knew I mustn't.

"*Ronde de jambe à terre*," said Miss Bedells. "Arms to first with the music, one and two." As the music started again, *dum, de de dum, dum, de de dum, dum, de de dum, dum,* I pulled myself up tight, clung to the *barre*, and focussed very hard on the girl ahead of me.

I could not concentrate. I thought of Mum and Dad so many thousands of miles away, across the Atlantic, across Canada in Vancouver. I vividly remembered their assurances. I was "the luckiest girl in the world" to get this opportunity, they said.

I straightened my back and held my chin high. I simply must succeed for them.

*Dorothea Campbell "Doffie" Sweeny*

# 1
## DOFFIE AND ME

*W*hen I was eleven years old, my parents sent me to England to live with my Aunt Doffie who had arranged for my training as a classical dancer. The year was 1933, and although I didn't understand it at the time, England was to be my home until my parents recalled me when World War II threatened. Being sent so far from my home in Vancouver came as no great surprise. Although daughters were not usually considered worthy of serious education in the families of either my mother or my father, it was traditional to send sons off to schools in England or Scotland. My father, in fact, had been enrolled in an English boarding school at age nine.

Aunt Doffie, Dorothea Campbell Sweeny, was my father's younger sister. I had not seen her since I was a small child. My memories of her during the years she had lived near us in Vancouver were of a vital and warm though sometimes overwhelmingly loud person of about twenty-five. Dimly I recollected her deep laugh, her powerful singing voice and the happy crowd of which she always seemed to be the centre.

The Sweeny family had been an important unit in Vancouver's social upper crust. In 1887 my grandfather, Campbell Sweeny, forty-one years of age and manager of the Halifax branch of the Bank of Montreal, had been assigned to "bring the bank west" and he set up the first British Columbia branch in Vancouver. In time, he expanded the Bank of Montreal to remote areas of B.C. and in 1912 was made superintendent for B.C. and the Yukon.

Grandfather Campbell Sweeny was as distinguished looking as he was gentle. He had been red-headed in his youth, but I only remember his snow-white hair, his full, upward-curving mustache and goatee. Tall, lean and very elegant, he was the perfect foil for my Nova Scotia Granny, Agnes Blanchard Sweeny. She had been known as "the Belle of Truro" when he married her, and her manner was somewhat grand.

When the small but classically beautiful Bank of Montreal building on Vancouver's Granville Street was completed, Grandfather and Granny took up residence—as was customary for the family of a chief executive at the turn of the century—in the spacious apartments above the public offices of the bank. Their private entrance was on Dunsmuir Street, and there, having summoned the man-servant by tugging on the long, embroidered bell-pull, visitors entered through a carved stone archway smaller than—but similar to—the main entrance of Ottawa's parliament buildings.

My grandmother received her guests in a setting of artistically deployed antique furnishings, carpets and velvet draperies. She was said to have been a formidable hostess. In social circles it was whispered that unless Mrs. Sweeny asked one to tea, one might as well leave town, but although some of her guests were recognizably important, just as many were colourfully non-conforming. Since Granny herself was a polished opera singer and gifted pianist, she especially enjoyed her opera visitors, the singers who came to town with famous touring companies.

Granny died before I came into the world, and eventually I inherited some of her lovely old pieces of furniture. A sepia photograph in my possession shows her with her hair piled high, her waist pinched and her hips bustled. It also clearly shows an heirloom bracelet—gold, with seven perfect cameos—encircling her wrist. This treasure is mine now and I wear it regularly with a pleasant sense of connection.

There were three Sweeny children. The eldest, my uncle, Sedley Campbell, was red-headed and six foot three when fully grown. My father, Sedley Fleming Campbell, had auburn curls and was six foot two. The name Sedley came from Granny's Truro family, but because of the ridiculous similarity of their given names, my uncle became known by the nickname Bimbo and my father by Ben (or "Benno" by my mother). Granny, determined that someone should carry on her family name, insisted my parents call their eldest son Sedley, "And use it!" And so my brother was stuck with this appendage for life.

Dorothea Campbell Sweeny, the aunt with whom I later went to live, was addressed with respect as Dorothea but usually answered to Doffie. Her portrait, Vandyke black except for a delicate Elizabethan lace collar framing the sad but beautiful face of a girl in her twenties, hangs over my fireplace today.

She was born with pure Titian colouring. From a very young age her squarish face with its delicate, creamy complexion was surrounded by a crop of coppery curls and ringlets. Thick lashes shadowed Doffie's twinkling brown eyes, set deep under finely arched brows. But her well-defined and sensitive mouth was at no time cherubic and far too early in her life took on, when at rest, a wistful sadness. Like her father and her two brothers, Doffie was built to be tall and lean, but at about the age of six something went terribly wrong. It became obvious that her spine had begun to twist. One shoulder drooped while the other was pulled up as though the muscles on that side of her neck and back had permanently contracted.

Once Granny was free to travel abroad, having shipped her sons (eleven and nine) away to boarding school, she took the young Dorothea to specialists in London, Paris and New York in search of a cure for what is recognized today as tubercular spine. At the same time she spread a story that Doffie was suffering from the effects of a fall onto "horrible concrete steps" below the Brighton pier; perhaps what the doctors were telling Granny was too painful to accept and it would certainly not have been proper to speak about. The "poor shrimp," as my mother called any child in trouble, suffered all kinds of indignities with braces and collars, and throughout her childhood and teens spent months at a time in hospitals in body casts with weights on her legs and her neck in traction. But nothing gave Doffie any relief from the pain that continued to attend the distortion of her body. In the end it had to be faced that she would always have a hunched back, uneven shoulders and twisted ankles, and that she would never grow to be more than four feet ten inches tall. Her suits and dresses would always have to be tailored to fit her odd shape and she would always need a walking stick.

Despite her physical difficulties, Doffie's spirit was impossible to quench. She became quite precocious and, though life was a struggle, she did her utmost to keep pace with it. Although athletics were not for her, she walked with determination and some speed. Encouraged by her devoted and tireless mother, she cultivated skills that would give her entry to the world of artists, although other than private tutoring in music and literature, extensive travel and exposure to visual arts, Doffie had no formal education. In her teens, however, she showed an unusual talent for singing. While travelling and living abroad with her musical mother, she learned Italian and became fluent in French as she trained with a succession of prestigious music teachers. With their expertise, her voice developed into a rich contralto showing a capacity for deep emotion—her own disappointment and grief ringing clearly from within a mountain of courage. Even as quite a young person, the full richness and wide range of her voice attracted the attention of several European maestros who, in spite of her pathetic appearance, one after the other took her on as a protege, only to give her up when they fully realized her limitations. Doffie's lungs had been partially squashed owing to the contortion of her rib cage. She was never able to sustain a powerful performance for a whole opera or even for a very long aria, and when tired, she developed an ugly cough. Because of her talent, however, she found the theatre world safe and rewarding. Artists in all fields, especially the authors of the time, became her lifelong friends.

While her parents were alive, she was always supported by them artistically and financially. Granny died in 1920, and after Grandfather's death in 1928, it was with the blessings of her two brothers that the small but comfortable Sweeny fortune was left entirely to Dorothea. Over the next four years she lived the flamboyant lifestyle of her artist friends wherever they happened to be. For this she needed more than the accrued interest of the estate and somehow managed to get her hands on a good bit of her "in trust" capital, though not always for herself. At times she helped her friends rather too liberally and found herself with neither cash nor credit.

When Doffie was "flush," the sky was literally the limit. I recall my parents reading aloud her letter after she had somehow managed to be the first woman to fly over the Andes. While living in Kenya, she wrote about several African safaris, said she had ridden on elephants in Rhodesia and complained about the discomfort of riding camels in Suez.

But Doffie's health, precarious at the best of times, was deteriorating. Bronchitis, which she referred to as "brown kittens," more and more often laid her low. Although there should have been plenty of money to provide her with good care, invariably when she was ill, there would be no cash in her account and no one looking after her. In 1932, the year I became ten, Doffie was living in Sydney, Australia, because her breathing seemed easier there. My parents wrote pleading with her to stop gallivanting and live more realistically. "If only she would settle somewhere and take an interest in someone," my mother would say, "she might be healthier and behave with more decorum."

My mother, Isabel Bell-Irving, and my dad had known each other since childhood and both served overseas in World War I. She had nursed in Lady Riddley's hospital as a V.A.D. (Volunteer Aid Detachment), and Dad, twice wounded, had led a company of Royal Engineers. Mother had lost her fiance, a Seaforth Highlander, early in the war, and she married Dad in England in 1917.

Considered a brilliant military engineer, Dad was offered positions at the Royal Military Academy, Sandhurst, and at the War Office as the war neared its end. He turned both down, accepting instead a posting to Murmansk, Russia, "because my friends are still fighting." Then in late 1919, Canadian Army Headquarters asked the British War Office to provide one of their finest engineers to act as an instructor at Canada's Royal Military College. When the War Office proposed their Canadian Sweeny as ideal for the job, Ottawa refused because he was one of their own. My sadly disillusioned Dad quit the service and brought Mum home to Canada with their firstborn, my brother Sedley. Back in Vancouver without a job, Dad gathered together a group of ex-army engineers, and as a company they did roofing, furnace repairing, drainage ditching and road building—anything to support their families. He even took a short-lived position as the safety officer for the Port of Vancouver.

Then much as he hated leaving his family in Vancouver, when nothing else turned up for him there, he accepted the position of development engineer at a mine in Anyox, B.C. Next he briefly worked as chief engineer for the B.C. Department of Highways. A job with the National Harbours Board as superintendent of construction for the Canadian National Pier ended when he was sacked by his Conservative superior because, not being a political animal, he had refused to fire his Liberal foreman of works.

In 1920 my brother Malcolm was born, and in 1922 Mum delivered me in the big bedroom of what we called our "green winter house" on Barclay Street, two-storeys-with-attic, sided with cedar shingles. I spent much of my earliest childhood in the neighbourhood of Beach Avenue and Pacific Street and remember the original bandstand at the foot of Harwood Street. The memorial fountain that now stands near there reminds me of Old Joe Fortes, the self-appointed lifeguard, saviour of many children. Behind the board fence that surrounded his hermitage at the water's edge, Joe kept a pony, and I could feel its warm breath and touch its soft nose through a crack in the fence.

I was six and my sister, Moira, three and a half when the house on Barclay Street was sold and the six of us moved into "the little house," an annex to Mum's father's house, "The Strands" on Harwood Street. Grandfather was the Vancouver industrialist Henry Ogle Bell-Irving. After our move, Mum spent much of her time caring for Granny, Marie Isabel del Carmen Beattie, who had been bed-ridden with arthritis for many years, and supervising the running of the Strands. While we lived there, my youngest brother, Roger, was born.

Meanwhile, as a very small child it appears that I had displayed a love of dance and something of a talent for showing off. Grandfather Bell-Irving, although an important businessman, was also a skilled figure skater. He and my Mum had enjoyed waltzing together when she was young, and several times before World War I he had taken her to Switzerland where everyone danced on the lakes. On one of his postwar sales trips to Europe for his Anglo-British

Columbia Packing Company, he had partnered the very young Sonja Henie, already on her way to her first world championship. Therefore, when I showed an aptitude at about age three, he taught me to skate, holding only the tips of my fingers, swirling me in wide circles on the open ice of Lost Lagoon, which in those days annually froze over. Then, so that his whole family could indulge themselves in this artistic sport, Grandfather built the Connaught Skating Club where the Westin Bayshore Hotel now stands on Georgia Street. All of his children and grandchildren had free passes. Grandfather Bell-Irving also paid for my dancing lessons, and in summer at the family retreat on Pasley Island he would invite me to dance for him and his long-suffering friends. I remember too that Grandfather had a Hupmobile and one of the earliest Chevrolets in Vancouver in which he drove his grandchildren around Stanley Park and right inside the giant hollow cedar tree.

When Grandfather Bell-Irving died in 1931, the Strands was sold. With five of us children to feed, and with Vancouver's cost of living climbing, Dad established us in a $12-a-month log cabin on the McKean's chicken farm at Gibson's Landing, a village up the coast accessible only by water, while he went job hunting in Vancouver. Ferry fares were too steep even in those days for many weekend visits, but how thrilled we were whenever the Union Steamship brought our Dad home.

Under these circumstances it was understandable that in 1932 my parents should ask Doffie for some of the inheritance Dad and Uncle Bimbo had so magnanimously given her, or at least for some financial help to educate her nieces and nephews. Doffie responded to Dad's letter with unexpected enthusiasm. She thought it was a great idea for her to pay for someone's education, but she didn't propose to send money.

"Dearest brother Ben," she wrote from Australia, "I have discovered the most wonderful dance teacher for your precious Verity. Could you bring yourself to part with her for a time? Allow me to take full responsibility for her care and development and bring to flower the great natural talent she has already shown so clearly. Deep in my heart I know, dear Benno, that you would not deprive your devoted sister of her nearest and greatest desire—to give Verity the

21

opportunity now, while she is the perfect age to become fully trained in her own special form of expression. . . ."

The letter must have come as a blow to my parents who had not considered careers for my sister Moira or myself. It would be difficult enough to educate the three boys. However, at least Doffie's offer would relieve them of one responsibility. It didn't occur to them to consult me, and for most of a year, letters travelled to and from Australia before I was given a hint about the plan. By the time it was actually in place, I was in Grade Five in the two-roomed schoolhouse at Gibson's Landing. Meanwhile, Doffie had returned to London because, she explained, Phyllis Bedells was *the only person* to train me. Phyllis had been Britain's first famous ballerina, then a teacher for the Association of Operatic Dance, later to receive a royal charter and become the Royal Academy of Dancing. She was, coincidentally, married to a distant McBean cousin of my mother. (Great-grandmother Bell-Irving had been a McBean).

In the spring of 1933, when I was finally told that I was going to live with Aunty Doffie, I was intrigued. However, I was not yet eleven years old and had never been away from home, and I could not guess how it would feel to leave my family or to be away for a long time. But to be allowed to dance was hugely tempting. I would be the luckiest girl in the world, my parents promised me.

And so it was decided. I celebrated my eleventh birthday on June 6 at the family cottage on Pasley Island, the idyllic summer retreat which by then was part of Grandfather Bell-Irving's estate. It lies in the mouth of Howe Sound, just west of Bowen Island, and in those days was two-and-a-half hours by small motor launch from Vancouver Harbour. I was given the whole of that summer there amongst my cousins to get used to the idea of leaving home.

It was also during that summer that Dad was hired for the thankless job of master at the junior house of St. George's School for Boys in Vancouver. Thankless, because he was expected to coach rugger and rowing as well as act as house master and teach religion, history, geography, math, art, physics and Greek. The pay was unbelievably low. However, the job had a few perks, such as providing gas for the great old touring car Dad bought to carry the rugger team to matches and the oarsmen to practice. It was known by everyone as the "Green Misery," and although it regularly carried far more bodies than was legal, the police forgave and forgave my Dad.

That September, since Mum was occupied moving our family from Gibson's Landing to North Vancouver and couldn't cope with the preparations for my journey, she sent me to her youngest sister, Beatrice Abercrombie. I stayed with her, except for one short visit to our new home, until it was time for me to leave Vancouver. Bea was the first adult ever to tell me to drop the Aunty part of her name. She was a favourite aunt, and at that time seemed to be quite rolling in her husband's money, spending it on the extravagant redecoration of their fine house near Southlands, a fashionable part of Vancouver. The bedroom in which I was installed was huge and elegant in softest blue and white. I had never slept in such splendour or comfort. Bea seemed to thoroughly enjoy preparing a wardrobe for my adventure, and the whole experience washed over me and into me like gallons of champagne. I saw my first-ever movie, *Birth of a Nation*, entered a department store for the first time and had my bouncy hair bobbed short in a "Beauty Shoppe." As a small child, I had been petite and dainty with long red braids, but when I was eight, Mum had been convinced by a woman friend that my heavy hair was sapping my strength and had sent me off with her to have it cut to shoulder length. It had frizzed. Now with this bob it seemed at last under control. Bea gave me my choice of pyjamas, dressing gown, underclothes, travelling dress, coat, hat, shoes and even gloves. But the very best were the stockings—brown lisle that had to be held up by four suspenders on a garter belt—which made all the difference between being a child and feeling like a grown-up.

Bea took me to various offices where she filled in pages of papers about me and my family At one place they took my passport picture, at another took my fingerprints. I had appointments with Doctors Spohn and Bricker, who were old friends, and saw a new doctor who was particularly concerned with my back and legs. For a potential dancer, I had what was considered a far from perfect body My bones had begun to enlarge, and though my arrns grew long, my neck didn't. By the age of ten, my short feet suggested I would never be tall, but already I had my father's big hands. My back was overly arched and my shoulders were definitely pronounced. To add insult to injury, my legs really hadn't been put on straight, and whereas my feet turned out fairly far, my knees didn't. My nose had become quite large for the size of my face—especially in relation to my small mouth which failed to hide protruding teeth. Though I had small, flat ears, I had invisible eyebrows and pale gold eyelashes.

When the October day for my departure arrived, Dad couldn't get away from St. George's School to take me to the train station in the Green Misery, so it was my mother's eldest brother, Uncle Henry, who came for me at Bea's house. It didn't seem especially strange to me then, though in retrospect it saddens me to recognize how often my parents were missing at critical times in my young life. Dad did tell me later that neither he nor Mum had been happy to let me go. Thinking back, I wonder if they had already said goodbye to more people than they had tears for.

At about half past five that evening, I stood on the platform alone in my rather adult clothes—a jaunty, green-trimmed brown velour hat, brown tweed winter coat covering a below-the-knees green wool dress under which could be seen my first-ever pair of long stockings and brown leather tie shoes—feet together, knees pressed back, chin out. Nearby, grown-ups chattered in small groups in the autumn greyness of Vancouver's Canadian Pacific Railway station at the foot of Granville Street.

In one of the groups, deep in conversation, was Dorothy Findlay, my Aunty Doffie's friend since childhood. She was known as Doffrey, which caused considerable confusion. Doffrey was a nurse and was on her way to spend at least a year in England taking postgraduate studies at St. Thomas' Hospital. It had been mentioned, quite casually, that we would be travelling companions since she was coming to stay with Aunty Doffie and me in London.

"'Board!" shouted the man in the navy-blue uniform with silver buttons. "All aboard!" A sudden tightness gripped my tummy as apprehension and excitement combined to speed up my breathing. I felt my chin quiver.

# THE SWEENY AND BELL-IRVING FAMILIES
## OF VANCOUVER

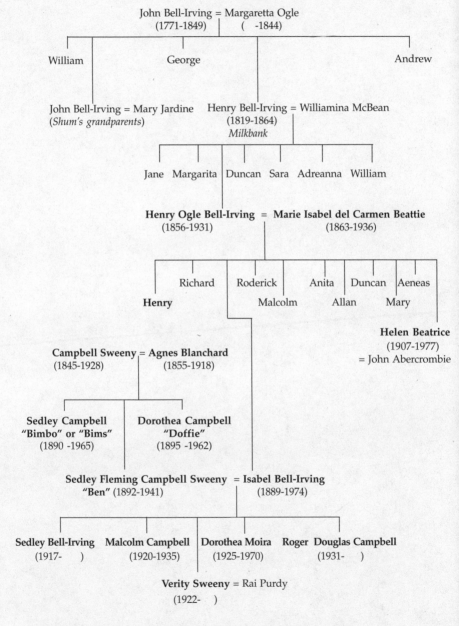

John Bell-Irving = Margaretta Ogle
(1771-1849)        ( -1844)

William     George     Andrew

John Bell-Irving = Mary Jardine     Henry Bell-Irving = Williamina McBean
(*Shum's grandparents*)     (1819-1864)
*Milkbank*

Jane   Margarita   Duncan   Sara   Adreanna   William

**Henry Ogle Bell-Irving** = **Marie Isabel del Carmen Beattie**
(1856-1931)     (1863-1936)

Richard    Roderick    Anita   Duncan   Aeneas

**Henry**     Malcolm    Allan    Mary

**Helen Beatrice**
(1907-1977)
= John Abercrombie

**Campbell Sweeny** = **Agnes Blanchard**
(1845-1928)     (1855-1918)

**Sedley Campbell**     **Dorothea Campbell**
**"Bimbo" or "Bims"**     **"Doffie"**
(1890 -1965)     (1895 -1962)

**Sedley Fleming Campbell Sweeny** = **Isabel Bell-Irving**
**"Ben"** (1892-1941)     (1889-1974)

**Sedley Bell-Irving**   **Malcolm Campbell**   **Dorothea Moira**   **Roger Douglas Campbell**
(1917-  )     (1920-1935)     (1925-1970)     (1931-  )

**Verity Sweeny** = Rai Purdy
(1922-  )

(The family members who appear in this story are shown in bold print.)

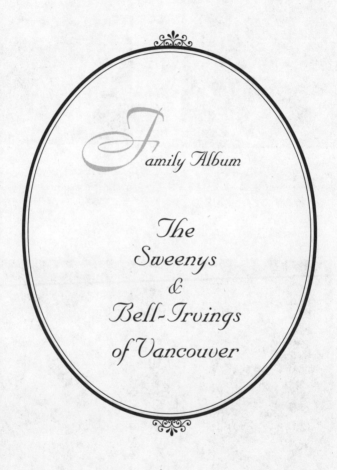

*Family Album*

*The*
*Sweenys*
*&*
*Bell-Irvings*
*of Vancouver*

Campbell Sweeny
Verity's paternal grandfather.
(1845-1928) c.1925.

Mrs. C. (Agnes) Sweeny
(nee Blanchard), Verity's "Granny
Sweeny." (1855-1918) c.1890.

From left: Sedley Fleming Campbell "Ben" Sweeny ; Campbell Sweeny
(Verity's paternal grandfather) ; and Sedley Campbell
"Bims" or "Bimbo" Sweeny c. 1912.

Mrs. H.O. (Marie Isabel del Carmen) "Bella" Bell-Irving (nee Beattie) Verity's "Granny Bell-Irving". (1863-1936). c. 1915.

Henry Ogle Bell-Irving Verity's maternal grandfather. (1856-1931) c. 1925.

The Strands, home of Henry Ogle and Bella Bell-Irving, was in Vancouver's West End, where they raised their seven sons and four daughters.

*Bella Bell-Irving, above with two of her daughters,*
*was confined to her bed with arthritis in later years.*

Dorothea Campbell "Doffie" Sweeny. (1895-1962) c. 1929.
She is wearing the "family pearls" which she pawned
during her frequent difficult financial periods.

*The wedding of Verity's parents,*
*Isabel Bell-Irving and Captain Sedley Fleming Campbell "Ben" Sweeny*
*in London, England, 1917.*

*Sedley Fleming Campbell "Ben" Sweeny with his children:*
*Sedley Bell-Irving, Verity and Malcolm Campbell.*
*1925.*

*Verity Sweeny aged about 3 years.*
*1925.*

*Verity and Dorothea Moira Sweeny play in a pool  on the top*
*of  Deer Rock on Pasley Island, west of Bowen Island, B.C.   1928.*

*Verity with younger sister Moira ( 7 & 5 years)*
*at family summer retreat on Pasley Island.*
*1929.*

*Isabel Sweeny, nee Bell-Irving, with four of her children:*
*Malcolm Campbell, Verity, Dorothea Moira, and Sedley Bell-Irving.*
*Vancouver, 1930.*

The Sweeny family at Gibson's Landing.
They are all wearing hand-me-down school uniforms, 1932.

Sedley Fleming Campbell "Ben" Sweeny with his family:
Malcolm Campbell, Verity, Dorothea Moira, baby Roger Douglas
Campbell and Sedley Bell-Irving. 1932.

# 2
## THE GUARDIAN

*N*ear me in another group the man standing closest to me but talking with grown-ups was Uncle Henry, a fierce-looking person whose dark hair and very dark eyes sometimes frightened me, even though I liked him. His questioning mouth seemed vulnerable and his voice was soft. Turning to me, he took my hand to hold me still while Doffrey said her farewells to the people who had come to see her off. I watched the porter help her and other passengers to board, offering them a hand to step onto a stool and then onto the steep metal stairs, four of them leading up to a landing where a door opened into the carriage. Now uncle walked me forward, giving my hand into the kindly porter's black one.

"'Evenin' Miss," he said, smiling a big white smile as he helped me climb to the top step.

Then the black man lifted the stepping stool and mounted the stairs, sending me back into darkness against a stack of cabin trunks which I knew included one of my own. When he had put away the stool and closed the low iron gate, I squeezed around him to lean on it and say goodbye again. My uncle watched me without smiling.

"All aboard! `Board!" shouted the porter once more, and he blew a scout whistle several times right near my ear. Reaching out, I grasped my uncle's shoulders.

"Goodbye," I whispered and, ashamed of my sudden teariness, tucked my head into his neck. "Take care of Mummy, please." My throat hurt.

"I promise," he said as he returned my hug, and then he pushed me away from him and stood back on the platform.

A moment later the whole train lurched with a clanking sound, then slowly began to move. I waved and waved as we had always done on Sunday afternoons at Pasley Island (both arms up, crossing and opening them) until the departing boat, which was taking our Daddies back to town, was completely out of sight. Then, just in case, we'd wave once more. This I also did, reminding myself, as I had been told, that I was the luckiest girl in the world.

The train picked up speed and, as the porter held open the carriage door, a blast of warm air dried the tears on my face. Everyone seemed busy making themselves comfortable, introducing themselves one to another. I found Doffrey about halfway up the car. With her feet up on the opposite seat, she was already reading a book.

"Well, there you are," she said.

"Did you think you had lost me, Aunt Doffrey?"

"For heaven's sake, Verity, drop that aunt nonsense. Have you something to read?" Her attitude was so casual you'd think we'd travelled together a dozen times.

"No, I haven't," I answered apologetically, "but I have a package to open if I may have my suitcase."

"The porter put it up there on the rack. His name is Jim."

"Oh! Of course, thank you."

"Wait till you see where you're going to sleep!"

"Where?" I asked, looking about with astonishment. It hadn't dawned on me that we'd actually go to bed on the train.

I reached up over the seat to pull down the smaller of two matching suitcases which had been the best of Aunt Bea's shopping treats. In it I knew I would find a gift from my friend, Coggie Buttar, who was a sister to Kathleen, my Uncle Dick's wife. Dear Coggie had no children of her own, but she cared very much about people and was adored by everyone who knew her.

Finding a shiny new key in the little purse that hung on a long string around my neck, I unlocked the two latches on my pristine case. Except for toothbrush, hairbrush and a pair of pyjamas, Coggie's package took up the whole space. Beautifully wrapped with tissue and ribbon, it gave me a Christmas or birthday feeling for a moment before I opened the attached card.

"Verity, my dear, may each day of your journey be filled with wonder. Remember I'll be thinking of you with love. Coggie."

Suddenly I wanted to cry, and I wished I hadn't packed my doll in the trunk. But I didn't cry and when the ribbon came undone, a whole bunch of small packages tumbled out. There was one for every day of travelling all the way to London. Each one had a little card saying on which day it should be opened.

With the mountains closing in, it was soon too dark to notice much of the scenery, but just being inside the lighted train speeding across the continent was thrilling enough for me. On that first night, the roaring, puffing, squeaking noises and the constant jiggling and swaying of the railway car took some getting used to, but they were all part of the great new experience in my life. The jostling journey forward to the dining car—pull open a heavy door, cross a cold and blowy joining section where the noise is double, then push through another obstinate door that slams behind you, shutting out some of the noise—was fun when you made a game of seeing how fast you could do it. Other children did it, too. Dinner that night—and every meal after that—was a treat with all the cutlery and shining glass and white tablecloths and the friendly black waiters who seemed to be there just to make everyone happy. They made quite an act of pouring under difficulties and never spilled a drop.

Bedtime became the highlight of every evening as Jim converted our sitting-up section into two spacious, comfortable beds. I stayed to watch while Doffrey went to sit with friends she had already adopted. Jim began by depositing a pile of linen on one of our seats. Then he grasped and unlocked a handle to pull down the curved, polished section of mahogany ceiling directly above our seats. And there it was, like magic, the upper berth. From this hidden cave he took out a stepladder, two heavy black curtains folded in squares, four pillows and two blankets.

"Watch this!" Jim pulled at his cuffs to show there was nothing up his sleeves. Next he drew a spring mattress halfway out of the cave and, balancing it on the edge of the upper berth, wrapped it in a snowy white sheet, tucking two top corners tight.

I laughed and clapped my hands. "You must be very strong!"

"Oh yes!" Grinning he added, "Making up three cars a night is good exercise." He flipped open a top sheet, folded the head end down over a wool blanket, tucked them tight onto the mattress and slid it back into place.

"You're so fast!"

"It gives me time for an extra cup of coffee." We went on chatting happily like old friends as he put fresh cases on two pillows and threw them deftly into position. Standing on the ladder which I would later climb to get into bed, he attached each curtain to a rod on the ceiling. Reaching between them, he switched on the little light in my berth. Then he removed the ladder so that he could make a lower berth out of the two seats.

Disappearing for just a moment, Jim returned with another pile of linen to make up an equally cosy-looking bed for Aunt Doffrey. He replaced my ladder and snapped the black curtains over her bed too. The whole sleight-of-hand took two-and-one-half minutes. Jim told me so.

Early on the first morning, having slept a little because I was truly tired, I awoke to feel the slow and laboured progress of the train. During the rumbly night I had discovered a slit of a shuttered window close to my head and through it watched the moon. Now I lay there looking at mountain peaks in a pink sky. Scrunching on my elbow and pressing my nose against the glass, I could see more shapes and get the picture of deep valleys. I began to realize how high up we were.

Catching sight of gift number one at the foot of my bed, I carefully unwrapped it. Not sure what I had found, I sniffed at the soft little sack, about four-and-a-half by six inches, and closed my eyes with delight at its scent. "Sweet dreams," said the tiny card, explaining the use of this balsam pillow. I slept with my nose on it for many years to come.

After breakfast, we went to the observation car. I could see the train with its two engines on a curve ahead of us and watched it take us into a tunnel. Acrid smoke, squealing brakes, unnerving bridges, precipitous ledges. The clackity-clack getting faster and faster. More climbing, slowing down, more descending, more bridges and tunnels. We wound around one mountain after another—deep snow, dry gravel

*The majesty of the Canadian Rockies has left a life-long impression on CPR passengers for over 100 years.*

slides, bare rock faces, sparse trees—and all of it swathed in silver-grey cloud against a sky that seemed so close there in the Rockies. There was snow on the platform at Banff, and the cold, dry air caught in my throat.

Another morning I awoke feeling the train purring along on a perfectly straight and level track. Opening my little view hole, I discovered a totally new world of blue and gold. No shapes, no shadows, just stubble and sky as far as I could see. So this was prairie! We came to farms, and once I saw a road running along beside the train track till it veered away. But flatness went on all day and was still there when I went to bed.

Then there were the lakes, thousands of small ones and some so vast they seemed to be oceans, and as the train curved around between them we went through forests, sometimes evergreen, although more and more it was brilliant deciduous bushes and trees that painted the landscape for me. Most impressive were the acres and acres carpeted in scarlet ground cover. We began to go through towns and more towns with their industrial areas of smoke and greyness, with farm country between and then more buildings. This is when I understood for certain that I was far away from home and still speeding on.

I had made some friends, but I spent a lot of time sitting alone, just gazing out of the window. Although she seemed far more interested in the other passengers than in me, Aunt Doffrey (it was hard to drop the "Aunt") turned out to be a good friend. In fact, she treated me as though I was quite grown-up and self-sufficient, speaking to me as an equal—an altogether new experience. I think this helped me to leave home with less concern than if she had treated me as the child that I was, already lonely and bewildered.

Very early on the fifth morning Jim's friendly voice boomed into my dead sleep. "Next stop Montreal! Breakfast awaits in the dining car."

Startled awake, I headed for the washroom as glimpses of red and yellow flashed by the windows. Autumn, as I had never seen her before, left me my clearest remembrance of Quebec.

A taxi took us from the CPR station to the docks on the St. Lawrence River. Although the Cunard liner, *Ausonia*, was only thirteen thousand tons, from where I stood on the dock below her great white hulk, she seemed to be the biggest ship in the world. When we had boarded and found our cabin with its upper and lower bunks, metal basin and port-hole several decks above the wharf, I immediately noticed a stuffy smell of paint mixed with disinfectant. Odour from the bag of oranges we had carried on board with us also thickened the air. I felt queazy.

When a steward came down our narrow corridor announcing lunch, I asked myself if I was hungry. I decided that food might help my tummy, but Doffrey wasn't in a hurry. She took her time brushing her short, black hair, powdering her nose and freshening her lipstick.

I prodded her, "Can we go to lunch now?"

"I guess you're hungry. Well, let's go. We'll need to find the purser's office to get the number of our table and find out which sitting they've given us." I sighed because my tummy was now growling.

Having climbed several flights of stairs, we lined up with others waiting to speak to the purser. After only a few moments Doffrey pulled me out of line saying, "Let's not wait around with that mob. We'll have a look around and find the main lounge. They are always pretty gorgeous on these ships." I followed her obediently. "There'll be a games room and a theatre."

And so we oo-oo-ooed and ah-ed at the shiny furniture, the heavy draperies, the sparkling light fixtures and the grand pictures of royalty. I'd never seen anything so formal and felt I had no business being there.

"Where's the games room, d'you think, Doffrey?" I imagined a sort of nursery, but it was just another large room with a lot of tables in it. The games, Doffrey told me, would be whist or horse racing. "Horse racing? How can they do that in here?" She pointed to a collection of cut-out horses on metal stands with numbers on them.

We never got to the theatre because at that point we went on deck to watch some little tugs, ever so far below, being attached to the side of the ship. Doffrey explained that the *Ausonia* was too big to manoeuvre herself away from the dock, but the tiny tugs would pull her out. At first they made a cloud of black smoke without moving anywhere, but after they churned up the water, the ship began to move sideways. I ran around to the other side where people were shouting "Goodbye" and throwing streamers back to their friends who shouted "Bon Voyage." There I discovered that the hawsers had, indeed, been let go and a space of water was growing between us and dry land. My hand felt the engine's vibration when it touched the rail. Returning to the port side, Doffrey and I watched the tugs. One pushed the stern in and two others pulled the bow out. Then the one at the stern let go and hurried forward, disappearing around the bow. The ship moved slowly out and forward. Soon our engines really throbbed, and as the small boats were disengaged, we moved rapidly into the stream of the St. Lawrence River. How funny it felt to look down onto the tops of buildings and to see, miles inland, fields and countryside bright with fireweed and autumn colours.

When at last we met the purser, he gave us a number and directed us to the dining room, at least five decks down. Doffrey quickly made friends with the six others who shared our table. Lunch was a feast, as were promises for all the meals to come.

Afterwards, Doffrey and I unpacked and wrote notes home. Then, determined to grow me up, she sent me off alone. "Take a look around. You can't get lost unless you fall overboard," she said cheerily. "I'm going to have a drink with the Dickensons. See you later." With that she left the cabin.

It didn't take me long to find the sundeck where I ran from bow to stern. Crossing from side to side, I watched the shores fall into shadow as the St. Lawrence widened. I could tell by the setting sun which direction was west, and that's where I was looking, leaning on the rail, when a man came and leaned beside me.

"Are you going home or leaving home?"

"Leaving," I answered with a lump suddenly in my throat. "Why?"

"You seemed to be a bit lonely and very small to be all by yourself. Where is home?"

"In Vancouver," I replied, hoping he would not go away.

"My! You are a long way from home. I was out there many years ago when I was a young man. I went to an island that belonged to an old man and his family. Do you know Isabel Bell-Irving?"

"She's my mother. Oh my goodness! You know her?"

"Well, I'll be darned. Isn't that something? Shows you what a small world it is. You know, it happens to me everywhere I travel. I run across people I know in the strangest places."

"Do you know her well?"

"Not that well, but we did go canoeing at that island."

"Pasley," I interrupted. "She has a kayak, too."

"You don't say," said the man, who seemed to be thinking far away. He didn't ask my name, nor I his. Soon he wandered off and left me thinking of home and what Mum might be doing right at that minute.

Dinner that night was another feast, but next morning, though Doffrey was in fine spirits, I awoke vomiting. The creak of timbers as the ship rose frightened me. The whoomph of ploughing into a heavy sea was not fun. My other problem was the smell. To me the cabin stank even with our porthole open, the salt air chilled me as I dressed, and the revolting odour of carbolic from visiting the toilet lingered in my nostrils. At the head of the stairs I knew I could not make it down to breakfast. Leaving Doffrey, I found my way back to the cabin. Putting on my coat, I dragged myself up several companionways to the promenade deck. Everyone out there had difficulty walking as the ship tilted first one way, then another. Seeing a steward, I asked (as we had been told to do) for a deckchair. Soon he had me tucked in beside a funnel, my feet up, head on a pillow, snuggled down under blankets, and he promised he would come again to see me. I shut my eyes but soon opened them because the sounds and movements made me dizzy. I watched people go by, lurching toward the rail as the ship dove into a trough, the sea coming up and the sky disappearing. Then I watched the people stagger inward as the sky dropped into the ocean, taking the horizon with it. Mesmerized, I locked my eyes in a stare for a few big rolls of the ship and then suddenly retched. I had nothing to throw up but I felt utterly miserable.

After several hours one of the ship's officers found me and literally pulled me out of my cocoon, insisting that I should walk and quickly at that. The officer said the only answer to seasickness was exercise, and that I must eat and drink fluids no matter how ill I felt. He held my arm and hurried me forward past one gushing air vent after another, but the ship's vents poured foul air up from the holds, up from the galleys, up from the engines, out of the washrooms and, worst of all, out of the smoking rooms. (Just thinking of stale cigar smoke sickens me to this day.) When we got to the bow or the stern, there were coiled hawsers reeking creosote. And there were people being sick by the rail while sailors mopped and threw down sand. I did my best, supported by the officer, but all I wanted was to lie down again. He tucked me into my chair and left. Shortly, a steward appeared with hot bouillon and Carr's tasteless dry water-biscuits. I stuffed them down as directed, but they came up again before I could get to the scuppers. More mops, more sand.

Hours later Doffrey came by and introduced her new friend, Roland. One on either side, they walked me several full circuits until it was lunch time, but I couldn't go down to the dining room.

"You'll have your 'sea legs' soon," Doffrey said.

I didn't. I couldn't bear the smells of the cabin or of food. I wanted to die. People stopped trying to make me walk, left me to huddle more and more alone as the weather worsened. One day, cowering under many wraps in my chair by the funnel, I realized we were not moving forward at all.

Someone who brought me a dry turkey sandwich explained about weathering the tail of a hurricane. The engines were slowed to the lowest they could go. "Just enough to keep her nose into it," he said. By that time almost all the passengers were ill. Even some of the crew found it exhausting and upheaved along with those few of us left on deck. For four days *Ausonia* rose, shuddered and fell groaning without making headway while the hurricane blew itself out. Except for the night hours when the ship's surgeon insisted I be returned to the cabin, I spent the remainder of the voyage on deck, very often the only person out there.

After fourteen days at sea, we entered the Thames estuary and steamed inland to Tilbury Docks. To have a steady deck beneath my feet was a relief, but I was tired and very wobbly. Even Doffrey said my face looked thin and pale. She appeared not to have suffered from the rough crossing. Because she had spent so little time with me, I figured my sickly condition had disappointed her, and I felt sheepish.

The October sky was grey, and a stubborn drizzle that began early had not let up by the time we docked around eleven that morning. We were ashore by noon, but it could have been four in the afternoon, or four in the morning for that matter, because everything looked so dark and depressing, especially under the metal roof of the customs shed.

As soon as we'd joined the customs queue, Doffrey handed me a bundle of documents and went off to find a telephone. I felt suddenly anxious about how to deal with the documents if the line moved quickly, but she returned just in time, spluttering, "How d'you like that? Dorothea's phone has been disconnected!"

I looked at her unbelieving. "It can't be. You must have the wrong number!" She didn't answer. The queue moved ahead. I must have looked the most wretched child as I stared up at Doffrey, desperate for her to produce some solution to our terrible problem.

"Well," she finally offered, "we'll just have to go to Chelsea and find her." She didn't seem worried so I took heart.

All our baggage had been piled up together, and when one officer had finished the paper work, we watched as another opened all our trunks and suitcases and dug about in them, then stuffed everything back, marking each piece with white chalk. Taxis were lined up waiting for fares outside the customs office, and one of the drivers, cap in hand, placed himself next to Doffrey. I couldn't understand a word he said, but Doffrey must have guessed the right signals. He piled our baggage on the taxi roof as well as beside him on his open air coachman's seat, and we two climbed into the dark passenger compartment of his little black box of a vehicle.

"Ware to, Muss?" said the driver, speaking to us through a little window he had opened beside his seat.

"Thirty-nine Cheyne Walk, near Battersea," said Doffrey.

"Ba'ersee wah'?" sniffed our driver. "We' gah' a lah' a Ba'ersees—Bwidge, Pahk, Plyce?—i' ul be the bwidge yer wants, innit?" Without waiting for a reply he pushed down a little flag on his fare meter, then spun the cab around in its own length, and Doffrey laughed hysterically as it rattled out of the building into hardly better light in a narrow street. Although I don't think Doffrey had been in London before, she seemed to be familiar with the districts, pointing out important buildings as we passed through the borough of Westminster. She must have studied a map. "Look at this, look at that!"

It didn't seem to bother her, but it did me, that the driver made so many twists and turns, left and right and right and right again, that we seemed to be retracing our route. When the street was narrow, he had to drive down the middle, but when on the wider streets there were cars going in both directions, he drove on the left! Doffrey apparently knew all about driving in England and was enchanted. But I couldn't see any fun in it. To me everything was old and crowded. All the houses were joined together. Everything looked dirty. Even the trees were black.

It took more than an hour, some of it spent stuck unmoving in city traffic-jams, before we got onto some wider streets and even saw the occasional tree. As we drove along, the rain ceased and the day lightened, and when Doffrey said we were on the Chelsea embankment, I guessed we were nearly there. We passed several little parks. Then between Albert Bridge and Battersea Bridge, we turned away from the river onto a cobbled street and within a block stopped, with two wheels up on the sidewalk, before an entrance clearly marked: 39 Cheyne Walk.

Without waiting for the driver to help us, we both scrambled out. I ran up a cement path between railings, up two steps to the recessed doorway and waited impatiently for Doffrey to catch up to me. She lifted and dropped the knocker. Silence. In a moment she did it again calling loudly, "Yoo-hoo! We're here! Anybody home?" Stepping back, we peered through a bow window into an empty apartment. My head swam as fear gripped me. Overly exhilarated and exhausted from seasickness, I clutched the railing to keep my balance.

Doffrey shouted at the driver who had been unloading onto the sidewalk. "Don't unpack us! We may still need you." He stopped and stood by his taxi.

Just then I caught sight of Aunty Doffie, jacket aflop and waving her stick, two tail-waving red setters criss-crossing in front of her as she rounded a corner, hurrying her crooked body down the middle of the cobbled street.

"Over here, darlings, over here!" she cried. "We've moved!"

At last the journey had ended. Instantly recovered, I ran to embrace Aunty Doffie.

We kissed on both cheeks and had a warm hug. "Hello, hello, dearest Aunty! We've found you!"

"Hello, dear things! How long you've been. Well! Well! Well! Gosh, it's good to see you both. I heard about the storm. I thought you'd never get here." She appeared so small to me, but then I had grown a lot in the four years since I'd seen her. There were tears in Doffie's eyes as she greeted her old friend Dorothy Findlay who, much taller than my aunt, wrapped her in a real hug. "Sure is good to see you, old girl. Long time no see."

Without thought for the taxi driver, we turned and, with my small aunt between us, walked arm in arm in the middle of the road the hundred or so yards back around the corner into Cheyne Row. We stopped because Doffie did at the small, dark green gate of Cheyne Cottage, Aunty Doffie's new home.

*Cheyne Walk. Even in the 19th century the classic history book, Old and New London, said, "The place from its air of repose and seclusion, has always reckoned among its inhabitants a large number of successful artists and literary celebrities." Joseph Turner, James Whistler, T.S. Eliot, and Ian Fleming all held Cheyne Walk addresses in different eras.*

# 3
## CHEYNE COTTAGE

Cheyne Cottage had been built on the fomer estate of Sir Thomas More, the statesman, writer and martyr who was executed by Henry VIII in 1535. The structure was originally a country hunting lodge or "shooting box" for King Charles II during his 25-year reign which began in 1660. It became part of the manor of Chelsea which was owned by Lord Cheyne at the close of the seventeenth century. Three hundred years later Cheyne Walk, Cheyne Row and the cottage still bear his name. As London grew, three storey buildings had pressed in against the shooting box on either side forming a stately row of residences, one the well-marked home of famed historian and philospher Thomas Carlyle. Their facades, snugged up to the sidewalk, formed a small courtyard in front of the set-back cottage. A privet hedge behind wrought iron railings enclosed Cheyne Cottage's little front garden of slate tiles and flower boxes. The cottage itself, built of brick, was almost completely covered with a very ancient grapevine. Above and behind the cottage I could see rooflines and chimneys. And I could see the sky.

My relief at having finally arrived immediately became enchantment as the three of us, plus the two dogs and a taxi full of baggage, stood before the cottage.

"This is it!" Doffie declared in a voice audible three blocks away. "Isn't it a poppet?"

First through the gate as Aunty unlatched it were the dogs who galloped across the tiny courtyard, up two stone steps and disappeared into the darkness beyond the half-

*Pen and ink drawing of Cheyne Cottage, Cheyne Row, Chelsea, London,
1933 as remembered by Verity Sweeny Purdy.*

open front door. Also painted a very dark, glossy green, this
door was heavy, panelled and trimmed with brass. The latch,
door knocker and postal slot gleamed as though polished
with love.

Doffrey stayed behind to deal with the taxi and our
luggage. As it was a very small house with a very narrow
entrance, Doffie led the way. I followed close on her heels
into the dim hall which was only three feet wide and not
more than eight feet long. A circular staircase, almost
hidden by the open front door, curved upward on my right.
Also on the right, another circular staircase curved downward. The entrance hall's only decoration was a slim, gilded
console ledge with a thin, tall mirror over it on the left wall
opposite the down staircase. Standing in front of the mirror,
Aunty pointed toward the wide archway on my left which
opened into a large and gracious drawing room.

I took one step inside. Angled out from its far wall was
a grand piano that dominated the room. Music—a continuing

part of my life—reminded me of Mum and the old nursery piano she had played for us at home, not so beautiful an instrument as this curved, black giant, but admired nonetheless for its mellow tone. To my left, a generous window showed me the garden again, and I could see an ornate metal bench, Victorian in style. From the window I could also look down into a square well, perhaps eight feet deep. Toward the bottom of it was a window that allowed the only natural light into the cellar room directly below the drawing room. Surrounding it were more trimmed privet bushes and a little iron railing. Directly opposite the front window, small-paned French windows stood slightly ajar, letting in some light from a room beyond. Under these windows stood an old teak sea chest, polished till it gleamed, and on it sat a large, square battery jar of pale green glass containing a mass of shaggy yellow chrysanthemums. Beads of light were captured in the bubbles of air clinging to their stems. On the hearth to my right sat the brass bucket, trivet and copper kettle I remembered from Grandfather Sweeny's house in Vancouver. Behind them a fire glowed, reflected on the broad waxed floorboards on which several faded Oriental carpets had been arranged.

Intrigued by the light coming from the French windows, I went into the next little room through an archway to the left of the windows. This room was not more than six feet wide! All it contained was a glass-topped cabinet holding a silver tray with several cut-glass goblets, a soda-syphon and a knife, and at the far right end of the room a sofa-bed completely filling the width of it. I found that the source of light was another window onto the back area, a sunken courtyard of many stone stairs and dark doorways. Looking up, I saw a design of chimney pots silhouetted against an angular corner of sky. Aunty had followed me into this slit of a room which she called "the bar."

"This is where the Duff-Arnotts sleep," she announced before opening another door to the one and only bathroom in the cottage. This, she explained, had been added onto the original building. The bathroom was another slit of a room. On the right, above a giant tub, it had one huge window that showed me as I looked down that this addition had been hung out over the sunken yard.

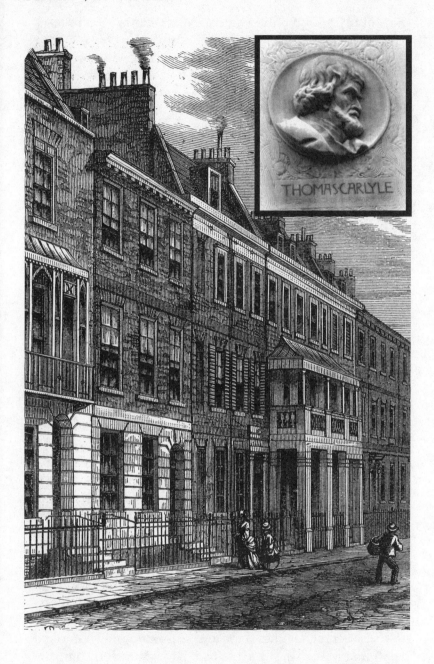

*Thomas Carlyle's statue stands in a small park where Cheyne Row meets Cheyne Walk. The Carlyle plaque (inset) denotes the Cheyne Row 19th century residence of Carlyle, only fifty metres from Cheyne Cottage.*

Aunty left me, closing the bathroom door, and I stood assessing the heavy odour I later learned was gas mingled with soaps, bath oils and dampness. A long chain dangled from a metal tank above the well-aged water closet or w.c. Lowering myself onto the cold seat, I looked around. Despite the fact that the hand basin was small and seemed to hang off the wall, there was an air of opulence about the room. Huge white towels were spread over warm pipes against the wall opposite the window, and several enormous bottles of bath salts and oil and dusting powder sat on the window's white-painted sill. The curvaceous bath tub, standing on its clawed feet, shone white. It had a large, single faucet below two huge brass taps. A strange tall tank stationed between bath and w.c. was attached to copper pipes, had a curved door and an on-and-off handle. A metal plate on its fat tummy declared its name to be "Thor." This was the "geyser" or gas water-heater.

The toilet paper was like shiny brown cardboard. I pulled the chain above the w.c. and jumped back as a noisy gush of water funnelled down a fat pipe into the bowl with its thick crust of deposited lime.

When I returned to the drawing room, our baggage had somehow arrived inside, taking up most of the entrance and spreading into the drawing room. I asked, "Who are the Duff-Arnotts, Aunty?" But Doffie was already leading me between suitcases onto the "up" staircase.

"P'tu! p'tu!" she grumbled (her polite substitute for *damn*), heaving herself up the steep pie-shaped steps against a curving wall. The wooden stairs and handrails were painted white, and the Oriental carpet runner, that had been skillfully folded to fit the curve, was fixed to each step with a brass strip. We arrived at the top of the stairs on a tiny landing and entered, on our right, an all-white bedroom. No, not all white. There was a bright Oriental carpet on the creaky, dark, polished wood floor, but everything else was white—walls, windowsills, panelled closets, chairs, bedspreads and convoluted ceiling. Two dormer windows spread light from north and south. I loved this room, bright carpet and all. Doffie told me which was her bed and which Doffrey's. Then she pointed out a cot in one of the dormers where Portia slept. Who was Portia? I said nothing, but already my brain connected Portia with the two red setters. I felt presences other than ours.

Doffie led me onto the landing again where two white panelled doors hid a cupboard of some kind. With one hand on each doorknob she pushed open the doors.

"Voila!" she exclaimed. "This is for my Verity!"

I stepped gingerly over a high doorsill into a green grotto. And a cupboard it was, but with its shelves removed. Its short wall and long slanted ceiling were painted the darkest, shiniest green I'd ever seen (or felt). I realized later on that it was the same green as the front door and the gate. A tiny dormer alcove held the smallest of casement windows with leaded panes. The remaining floor space was exactly the length of the child's bed which was against the green wall, leaving a small patch of warm carpet to stand on. Doffie explained that I could hang a few clothes behind a little print curtain.

Over my bed, where the back wall became slanted ceiling, a very narrow shelf—not above my shoulder when I sat up in bed—held an assortment of creatures. I could tell at a glance they were all treasures. Beneath the window stood a miniature mahogany chest of drawers and on it was Aunty's most friendly and joyful gift—an explosion of anemone, blue, purple, pink and scarlet with startling black centres, that took up most of the top of the chest. The flowers seemed to say, "Welcome to your new home, your own place, your private world." I buried my face in them, then sat on my bed, weeping. Doffie said nothing, but her eyes told me she understood my feeling of being overwhelmed.

At this very moment both dogs pushed past my aunt and leaped into my space. They were all over me, wagging and licking, on my bed and off, jumping over each other. As fast as they came, they went. Doffie followed them.

"Come down when you are ready, my sweet," she called back. "Breakfast won't be long." I was sure my aunt must have meant lunch!

After she left, I closed my doors in order to feel the full size of my domain. While open, they had partially concealed my chest and flowers on one side, and the little curtained cubbyhole on the other.

I looked for a long time at the carved animals and birds

*Verity's pen and ink drawing of the "cupboard bedroom" in Cheyne Cottage, Cheyne Row, Chelsea, London as it was in 1933.*

I assumed were now mine—the three pink elephants on their small ebony stand and two black elephants standing side by side, the heavy brass jackdaw, sheep, goat and camel carved from sandalwood, and several ivories. Having taken each one in my hand, examined it and replaced it carefully, I took the last and most enchanting gift in both hands to turn and admire its exquisite ivory carving. Not more than five inches tall, including her pale jade pedestal, a wee girl in a smock stood on her tiptoes. Her two long braids were tied with fat ribbon bows and her fingertips touched her skirt. I knew she was me as I had been short years ago when my braids reached the hem of my smock. Tenderly, I put her back and took a long, long look out of the faerie-tale window, past our vine-draped chimney, across the roof tiles and up, up to other roofs and a myriad of chimney pots. Peter Pan was out there somewhere. I was sure of it.

I didn't have to be told there was food downstairs. The smell of it wafted into my room as Doffrey opened my cupboard doors. "So here you are," she said, leaning into the greenness and looking about. "It's not very big, is it?"

Turning to show her my new animal friends, I hit the corner of the shelf with my shoulder, dumping them around me. "Oh! No!" I leapt from the bed to gather them up. "Oh no!"

"Come on down," she said, making no effort to help. "We've got kippers for lunch."

"Kippers? What are kippers? Is that the smell? Ugh-h! I don't feel much like eating that smell." However, steadier on my feet now and hungry despite my dissenting nose, I left my room, carefully closing my doors behind me. Heading toward the sound of laughter from below, I felt my way cautiously down one rounding staircase to the entrance hall, then down the other through thickening smoke and odour, coming at last to a cobblestone floor. This was the dining room, dark and echoey and cold.

Pale daylight, coming down the shaft from the garden, entered through a small window in the thick stone wall of this dungeon. The daylight was slightly augmented by the glow from a standard lamp that was reflected from the surface of an ancient, black oak dining table and chairs, from glasses, cutlery and from blue-and-white china. Warmed by their aperitif, neither Aunty Doffie nor Doffrey Findlay seemed aware of anything but happy days gone by. Bending over a low gas grill at the bottom of a rough brick chimney, they bickered good-naturedly about how high the flame should be. They hadn't seen me.

"Hello! I'm here!" I announced.

"Well, so you are," said Doffrey.

"My sweet Verity," said my real aunt, "kippers are nearly ready. Come along, I'll show you the kitchen." I followed her past the oak dining table and turned right through a doorway where the uneven cobblestones definitely sloped downward. Inside the kitchen there was even less natural light as only one small window let in a little daylight from the area which I had seen from the bathroom. The glare of a couple of bare bulbs on wires shone on the dark kitchen walls where ancient pots hung from hooks. A four-ringed gas burner stood on the high side of the floor; a sink of sorts and a butcher's table completed the decor. Aunty Doffie took me through a door of rough boards with a lift-latch which led out into the area. There she indicated another rickety-looking door at the top of stone steps opposite. This was the extra loo— "primitive to be sure, my sweet." She pointed out another door next to it that led through a stone wall into the lane. The coal shed was under the bathroom and beside it was a cooler where, on a slate counter, cheese and such were kept under heavy covers because of the rats and mice.

Back in the dining room, Doffrey had served up the kippers and I was told where I should sit. I don't know what they were drinking, but my aunt offered me some barley water with lemon.

"I'd like to try it, please."

"Want some soda in it?" asked Doffrey.

"I don't know. I've never tasted soda. P'r'aps it would be nice, thank you." She mixed up a concoction at a little table in a dark corner and I jumped up to get it.

I had to watch to find out what to do with kippers which I could see were fish, but fish full of hairy bones. I saw Doffrey open her mouth to put in a large forkful of kipper with bones hanging from it in all directions. Stop! Stop! I wanted to shout, but I never formed the word. The mouthful went in and Doffrey chewed as though it was delicious. What's more, my aunt did the same thing. Pulling some of the offenders out of the corner of her mouth, she munched away as though in heaven.

I hesitated before asking, "Can you eat the bones?"

"Of course!" said Doffrey, stuffing her mouth again. "It would be impossible to eat kippers without bones. They don't fillet them. That's half the charm."

I managed to separate a few morsels that seemed hair-less and swallowed them despite an argument with my throat. Toast, rather badly burned on the grill, and some bitter marmalade filled my emptiness. I couldn't finish the insipid barley water and was glad my offer to do the dishes was immediately accepted by both. As they went upstairs, one of them said, "Give the dogs the remains." Cinderella had set herself up.

We were all in the drawing room later in the day when Mr. and Mrs. Duff-Arnott and their daughter Portia—about five years old—walked into the house. After the dogs—which turned out to be theirs—made a fuss over them, Aunty Doffie introduced us all.

It seemed that Doffie had rescued this family—quite charming but altogether hapless—and was putting them up until one or other of the adults got a job. Beverly was an actress, Joe, a writer. Portia attended, thanks to Doffie's largesse, the local kindergarten. They had all been out on an unsuccessful job hunt. Bev and Joe dropped their coats on their bed and poured themselves drinks in the bar.

"Can I get anyone anything?" asked Joe.

Whose house is this, anyway? I wondered as I found a corner to sit in. Having filled their glasses, the adults chatted standing up. I watched their gestures of familiarity with astonishment, hardly noticing Portia who shared the company of the dogs with me.

"Where do the dogs sleep?" I asked.

"In the bar usually."

"When do you go to bed?"

"I don't know. After dinner, I think."

"Who makes dinner?"

"Everybody."

"Have you ever been on a big ship for days and days?"

Although I tried to be nice to Portia, I was really keeping one ear on the adults' conversation. Once I thought Doffrey was laughing about my being so seasick. "Had everyone visiting her on the deck," I heard her say, as well as other bits about our journey.

Portia insisted I go upstairs to see her new doll, and there I saw, sitting on her cot, Angelina Sarafina Sarah Mackintosh. Oh, if Aunty had given Angelina to Portia I would be sad! Angelina had been Aunty's friend since she was a little girl, and when I was very little I had played with her on the window seat of Doffie's big bedroom in Vancouver. As it turned out, Angelina had only been lent to Portia, and many years later she became mine. I still have that old black girl— a white-faced doll covered with black silk, with slits in it for her china eyes—and all her handmade skirts and apron and petticoats and sun hat. She once had hands with sewn fingers and feet with sewn toes. I'm sad to say that in later years my own little granddaughter didn't treat Angelina very well. Now wrapped in a soft old linen pillowcase she is safe, but the stuffing has come out of those fingers and toes.

Doffie's voice from below wakened me from a reverie.

"Come along down, children, we're all going to the Blue Cockatoo for dinner."

"Yes, Aunty. We're coming right away." I got my coat and hat from my cupboard and hurried down the winding steps with Portia on my heels. I needed to use the bathroom but people blocked the way. I hadn't tried the loo outside and felt quite scared about going through the dungeon in the dark, so I crept through the drawing room and the bar and, to my relief, found the bathroom empty.

The Blue Cockatoo was just along the embankment from Cheyne Walk toward Chelsea Bridge. It was a little place, down two steps from the sidewalk to a patio where painted wooden birds hung in trees planted in holes in the pavement. Tall people had to duck to avoid the branches. In the tallest tree a neon cockatoo, pale blue with a yellow tuft and yellow beak, advertised this eating place. Inside, the restaurant was softly lit and a fire burned. The food was good, simple but tasty, and the portions were just what a growing person needed. It was Doffie's favourite restaurant and she always knew some of the people there. It wasn't rowdy, but people did talk across the room and from table to table. It felt very friendly.

When we got home after dinner that very first night, everyone announced what they wanted for breakfast. Unsuspecting as any willing child and forgetting about the dungeon, I offered to make it for all of them.

What seemed fun at first—despite the odd mouse among the dirty dishes—soon lost its glamour. I cleaned up after the grown-ups, made the kitchen respectable, provided breakfasts and emptied ashtrays. I even shopped for cigarettes, newspapers and sometimes alcohol. I became expert at lighting cigarettes—"Hold the match high so you don't singe their eyebrows"—pouring drinks—"Bev likes a little gin and a lot of tonic, de Beezer doesn't take soda in her scotch." I learned to recognize when someone had had enough and the trick of pouring their next drink light. I answered the phone: "This is Miss Sweeny's niece, Verity. May I say who's ringing?"

It seemed ages before anyone mentioned dancing. Then one Sunday, Aunty focused on me. In an unusually business-like way she announced, "Today we are going to meet Miss

*Phyllis Bedells (McBean) (centre) in performance c. 1930.*
*She was Britain's first officially recognized ballerina and head of*
*the Phyllis Bedells School of Dancing in London where Verity*
*received her dance training from 1933 to 1936.*

Bedells, and tomorrow your governess, Miss Richardson, will
be here at nine to begin your schooling. You will need some
books. I'm sure she will take you shopping."

At about four that afternoon our taxi drew up at the first
door of an impressive block of stone houses in Maidavale.
They had been built, as were most London houses, with a
common wall between dwellings. Wrought iron railings, like
a row of cages, separated the properties from each other and
guarded stairs that led down to open areas and secondary
entrances. Iron rails beside stone steps led up to each of the
front doors. They were all alike except for a number.

The door bell was answered by Miss Phyllis Bedells
herself, and Aunty greeted her as though she had always
known her. I was told to call her Aunt Phyllis—for politeness I thought—and had no idea for at least a year that she

was, indeed, family. It hadn't been explained to me that Miss
Bedells was married to my mother's cousin and was really
Mrs. Ian McBean, although she still used her maiden name
as a dancer and teacher. I would, of course, be expected to
call her Miss Bedells at school.

My new aunt showed us to her drawing room where a
coal fire burned. I well remember that room. It was high-
ceilinged and generously furnished with big soft chairs and
a sofa covered in Sanderson chintz. The carpet was cream-
coloured with a gentle floral pattern and had thick fringes at
each end. To close out the dusk, Aunt Phyllis unhooked the
wide ties which held back heavy curtains from the windows.

"Sit down, my dears," she said, offering me the big chair
opposite hers before the fire. "So you want to be a dancer.
We'll see what we can do." Just then a maid brought tea,
which gave the women time to talk, mostly about Australia
as I recall, while I looked about the room and grew to feel
comfortable in the presence of my teacher.

After tea, Aunt Phyllis told us that her method of teaching dance was the rigorous Royal Academy technique.
Developed in Britain, the Royal Academy became the foun-
dation for the famous Royal Ballet. The grown-ups discussed
the syllabus which included five children's grade exams for
beginners like me, to be followed by elementary, intermediate and advanced exams that would take at least a year each
to complete. In addition, there were professional and teachers'
examinations. Aunt Phyllis explained the difference between
pupils, who might dance for an hour or two a week, and
students like me who planned to become professional and
danced every day.

"Every day, Aunt Phyllis?" I repeated, astonished.

"Yes, my dear, every afternoon except most Saturdays
and Sundays until you finish with your governess. Then it
will be all day every day." It was rather hard to get clear in
my head that I wouldn't be going to regular school at all.
My age was just right to begin serious dance training. Start-
ing too young, my teacher told us, was frowned upon by the
Academy and its qualified teachers.

"Although it may seem logical to take advantage of the
extreme natural flexibility of young bodies," she said,
"X-rays have proved that deep back bends and *pointe* work—

without having first developed strong back and leg muscles—have done irreparable damage to spines and feet." It was sheer good luck that I was eleven when my real dancing began.

I don't remember much else that Aunt Phyllis said, but I do remember her taking my bare right foot in her left hand. With her right hand she held my toes and pushed them upward as far as they would go. Holding the heel, she gently but firmly pressed my foot down and stretched it, pulling out my curled toes until they were flat. Then lightly, with the tip of her finger, she traced my instep from beginning to toe and, looking at me in a kindly way, said, "My, we have a long way to go, haven't we?" She slipped off a dainty shoe to show me her own stockinged foot with its fine arch and perfect point. It didn't look a bit like mine. When we left, Aunty had a list of instructions and a calendar for the balance of the term. We'd meet again in eight days, Aunt Phyllis said.

At 8:45 the following morning, Aunty was up and dressed and waiting for me in the drawing room. She had pulled back the curtains and opened a window. Neither of the Duff-Arnotts were in evidence. Someone had made their bed and puffed up the chair cushions.

"Good morning, my sweet," sang out my overly cheerful caretaker. "Are you ready to put on your thinking cap?"

"My thinking cap? Will I need a thinking cap, Aunty?" I said, giggling to match her gaiety. I popped a morning kiss on her cool cheek. "Will Miss Richardson be awfully strict?"

"To be honest, I haven't the vaguest notion. Shirley Radford found her for me. But we'll soon see.'

I can't imagine where Aunt Shirley (wife of the British actor of note, Basil Radford), my aunt's dear friend and soon mine, found the governess who arrived that morning and most weekdays after that to teach me. Miss Richardson gave me the impression of having come from another time. Her teeth were held together by clips and strings that caught food. Whenever she spoke to me, she held the sharp tip of a pencil against her lip or between those rickety looking teeth. Not only did she seem elderly, the clothes she wore were old-fashioned as well. A white blouse had a high collar with a ruff which covered her wrinkled neck and caught the untidy wisps of tinted hair that tried to escape from the little knot at the nape of her neck. Her high-waisted, ankle-length skirt covered thin legs, and high-tied oxfords gaped around bony ankles.

The subjects she taught—a little of this and that including Greek mythology, Greek architecture, religion, art, French and music—seemed to lack some of the essentials that even Miss Ingles had taught at the elementary school when we lived in Gibson's Landing. I still have a drawing book filled with pictures—Miss R drew and I coloured—of Corinthian pillars, wise men, the Mount of Olives, kings and queens and Stonehenge. It remains a pathetic reminder of the inadequacy of my education. We spent about three hours each morning reading from worn old books, parsing French verbs, repeating musical scales and colouring. At noon she disappeared. Within that first week I felt I knew her well.

After a lunch of sorts, it was time for Aunty to take me by taxi or by bus—depending on her finances—to ballet school. During that first week, Doffie had found a seamstress and persuaded her to make my tunic, a simple blue silk shift with matching briefs. There was a pattern for the shift, and they got that quite well, but what they gave me to wear under it would have fit a wrestler. Hugely full, gathered in with elastics to make balloons of my buttocks, my knickers held the tunic away from my body, making me look ridiculous. What could I say? I had no choice but to appear so dressed for my first lesson. "P'tu, p'tu," Doffie fussed as she put on her coat and hat and foraged for a walking stick at the back of the very small closet. "Come along, Child. We'd best get a taxi." Off we set to Maidavale.

Wearing my little black slippers held on with elastic, I followed the other children (with Aunty tagging along behind) upstairs from the dressing room and into a room called a studio. This room was big, a bit like a gymnasium with windows at either end. Halfway along the far wall was a small alcove where the floor was raised one step. On it was a piano and sitting there to play music was an elderly woman. As I came in, a lady caught my hand and said, "I'm Edna Slocombe. Please come with me, Verity. I shall introduce you to Mrs. Bedells, Miss Bedells' mother. She plays the piano for us. " Miss Slocombe led me across the room toward the outstretched hand of dear Mrs. Bedells who took my hand in her soft, warm one and held it while she welcomed me, smiling all the while. We were to become good friends.

Miss Slocombe then showed me to a place near the piano. There I could hang onto the *barre*, a rail which ran all the way around the room except across the door, the piano and the end where Miss Bedells stood against the back window, watching us all. She smiled at me and waved a hand slightly, letting me know she remembered we had met before.

Looking about, I could tell that the other children already knew a lot of things. Later I learned that most of them had started a month before me. They knew their places and the way to stand with their left hands on the *barre*, their heels together, their knees straight, and their toes pointed out. I tried to copy them, but when I put my heels together my knees wouldn't go straight. Not only that, my toes didn't want to go very far out and I realized that my tongue was hanging out with the effort.

"This is dancing?" I asked myself, and then Miss Bedells was speaking. "Positions by *dégagé*. Arms to first with the music, one and two." Somehow I got my right arm to the side (though it soon fell down) and tried my best to follow what the others did with their feet. *Dum, de dum, de dum, de dum,* Mrs. Bedells played on her piano. One foot only did the moving around while the other tried to stay turned out and not wiggle. Four times they started out to that *dum, de dum, de dum, de dum,* and I was just beginning to see the shape of it when they pulled their hands up high and swizzled around to face the other way.

"Arms to first. One and two," said Miss Bedells again. "Hold the *barre* lightly and keep your heads up!" This time she moved along the line of girls near her, lifting a chin, placing an arm properly, pushing a behind in, then a tummy in, but that didn't stop anybody from doing the *dum, de dum, de dum, de dum* movements with their feet until it was time to "pull up in fifth position and *détourné*" once more. While waiting for the next exercise the girls stood still with their toes turned out and kept their hands low in front of them. Miss Slocombe, who was also helping here and there, soon came to guide me. She rounded my elbows and showed me how to curve

*Portrait of Aunty Doffie when she was about 20. c. 1915.*
*This portrait hangs over the fireplace in Verity's home.*

my fingers gently toward each other. Then she put both her hands on my shoulders, softly pressing them down.

Next came *tendu*, a stretching of the foot. "Right foot stretch forward, then close, then to the side, and close, then to the back, and close, and to the side again." Miss Bedells demonstrated as she spoke and Miss Slocombe put herself between me and the piano, ready to do the exercise in front of me.

After that came *pliés* on each side, then *battements*, small ones first, then higher ones. Throwing the leg, swinging the leg, and *frappés*, knocking the leg. It went on and on, first one side, then the other, with different music for each kind of movement. All the while I was expected to keep one arm

67

outstretched beside me just below shoulder level. My arm ached. As the *barre* work continued, the shoulders and head were to be used, leaning toward the arm and away from it. I was highly confused and wished I could sit and watch for a bit. But, no. Aunty had the only seat.

After a time we moved to the centre of the room to positions in rows of four. I was put fairly far back behind a girl who knew the exercises well. I learned later that many of the girls were not actually beginners and that students at all levels took several classes a day, including this one for beginners. Hours counted just as much as the level of technique.

Centre practice, which started with the five positions of arms, was completely baffling. It seemed that it was just one long flailing around that I couldn't get the hang of at all. Something with the knees bending and stretching and a lot of little jumps was followed by running, hopping, skipping and rushing from one corner of the room and leaping into the other corner.

At the end of an hour there was what Miss Bedells called a "thank you" movement, known as a curtsey. I knew what a curtsey was, but theirs wasn't like mine. Oh, my head was tired. But Miss Bedells came and put her arm around my shoulder and told me I did finely for my very first time. At that point I wasn't at all sure I wanted to be a dancer.

Standing beside Aunty Doffie while she chatted with Miss Bedells, I was relieved to hear that my knickers should be considerably cut down, and on the way home Aunty Doffie promised me that the lady who made them would come back to "fix my breeks." I was horrified to hear that I must wear woollen tights to keep my legs warm while dancing as well as travelling to and from school. Aunty said she would knit them. I thought of them as ugly, itchy and juvenile, but later, when I saw the "big girls" wearing knitted tights, I grew to appreciate them and to be grateful to Aunty for taking on this enormous task, not once but many, many times. I was one of the lucky ones because she could knit.

Doffie was very keen for me to shine in every endeavour, French in particular. With this in mind she tutored me furiously and with much sarcasm at every possible opportunity—in theatre queues, in restaurants, in taxis and on busses.

I was embarrassed and wasn't a good student. We caused amusement everywhere we went, especially since she was always knitting. Even if the seats we had on a bus were not together, she'd begin a lesson, interrupted only when she needed my help to untangle wool—across an aisle yet!—muttering "sacre nom de Dieu" and other oaths under her alcohol/nicotine breath.

As soon as I started my dancing lessons, Doffie insisted that I go to bed early. This usually meant having to pass through her guests to the bathroom in my pink dressing gown. After my bath I went straight to my room where I had to wait for my supper and eat it from a tray in bed. It was difficult to keep the dogs from stealing my meal because they simply pushed the doors open and came waggling in.

We sometimes went to school by bus, Doffie and I, long after I knew my way and could have managed. Though she huffed and puffed and swore a lot, she insisted on taking me—perhaps she had made a promise to my father never to let me travel around London alone. Getting to school was a lengthy and often hectic adventure, never without traffic-jams and often fog. Frustrating as it must have been for Doffie, it was more deeply so for me because I hated being late—which we almost always were. We were never late because of me; I was up before anyone else to make breakfast. But the grown-ups, who always went to bed very late, found it hard to wake up. Once I missed a whole class. At school they must have known it was not my fault because no one ever scolded me about it, but I felt ashamed always being the last student to enter the studio. Sometimes Doffie was so late picking me up after school that Miss Bedells came down to get me from the empty dressing room. Embarrassed and weary, I developed hiccoughs that often lasted for hours. To add to my embarrassment, several warts that had been on my hands as long as I could remember had begun to spread.

I made some lasting friends at Phyllis Bedells' school, one of them being her daughter Jean who, I discovered at last, was my second cousin. Jean was already a good dancer when I arrived and she went on to become ballet mistress to the Royal Ballet and senior adjudicator for the Royal Academy. Mary Sterling and Phyllis Dakin, neither of whom were studying seriously, were the two "best friends" I gained from going to dancing school, and both had "normal" families who welcomed me from the beginning. Although Aunty obviously approved of them enough to allow me to visit their homes, neither of them ever came to the cottage.

To me, Mary was extraordinarily beautiful, combining the almond skin-colouring, slanted eyes and full lips of her elegant Chinese mother and the aristocratic good looks of her English father, an accomplished artist whose paintings hung in the Royal Academy. Mary was tall. Her hair, heavy and straight, was as brown as her eyes, and at thirteen she already had grown-up breasts. Her legs were long and very straight, if slightly shapeless. I have no idea why she liked me. The Sterlings lived on the third floor of a western-style apartment building in Maidavale. Mary's mother maintained her Oriental customs of dress and food preparation, although she was the only one who ate the special foods set apart on a sideboard beside a pile of little dishes; she was the first person I ever saw using chopsticks. Occasionally I shared Mary's spacious bedroom and her large bed. Having no plans for a career in dance, she told me, with delightful openness and clarity, her expectations about marriage and having children. I couldn't help feeling twinges of jealousy and homesickness.

Phyllis Dakin lived with her mother Violet, sister Sylvia and brother Tony in an elderly row house on the embankment at Bedford, two bus rides and a train ride away from Phyllis Bedells' school. Captain Dakin, posted to the Middle East, was rarely present and I quickly became aware that Mrs. Dakin was happier when he was not, life being tough enough bringing up the children without his interference or the various British foreign service influences that came home with him. She was motherly, blowsy and untidy. So was Sylvia. Tony, plump and pale, went to a Bedford day school for boys, and Phyllis, who must have left school at thirteen, was popular with all the chaps Tony brought home.

I envied almost everything about Phyllis. Willowy and clothes-conscious, she had a large room of her own that was decidedly feminine. She had her own records and record player, and framed photos of young men adorned her bedside and dressing tables. Phyllis wore a little make-up and the odd bracelet and dressed her fine, fair to mousy, shoulder-

*Cheyne Cottage, Chelsea, London, in 1997. The red brick home sits unnumbered between 14 and 16 Cheyne Row.*

*The Kings Head & Eight Bells pub has marked the entry to Cheyne Row since the street was built in 1708.*

length hair in any number of attractive ways that never stayed put for more than a few minutes. Although she was generally lethargic, she was animated around boys. I doubt she could ever have made a professional dancer.

Although I was not allowed to go anywhere on a bus by myself, on my odd afternoons off I was permitted to visit small parks along the embankment. Those boundaries gradually enlarged as my curiosity led me into private parks with gates that were locked at night and, as I investigated inviting lanes and shortcuts leading away from Cheyne Row, I came across small shops on side streets that really intrigued me. One in particular, that sold tiny knitting needles and the smallest balls of wool I'd ever seen, became the recipient of my erratic but sometimes generous weekly allowance. Over time, with enthusiastic help from Doffie, I provided my doll with an entire wardrobe of skirts and jumpers, dresses, coats and hats, an occupation that kept me happy and busy for many hours in my cupboard. It no doubt suited the grownups who seemed to sleep as often as possible during the day.

One Sunday morning when I was out alone, I found most of the park gates locked so I returned early from my walk. As I approached Cheyne Cottage from the north, I could see fog rising from the Thames. Entering the cottage, I headed for the bathroom only to be stopped in my tracks. Mr. and Mrs. Duff-Arnott were laughing hilariously as Aunty Doffie came out of the bathroom stark naked! Fresh from her bath, not even a towel to cover her pulchritude, Aunty seemed to be parading—until she saw me. I turned quickly to avoid her eyes and ran upstairs to my cupboard.

"How could she?" I could hear my mother's voice full of disgust and condemnation. "Has she no shame? Her body all crooked and soggy pink fat! Ugh!" I had been taught that one shouldn't uncover oneself publicly, especially when what one had to show wasn't pretty—but in front of a man?

Why were they laughing? I couldn't figure it out. Of course, I had pretended not to see her and tried to forget that I had, but the questions kept tumbling about in my head. Why would she do that? What had made them laugh? What secret had I stumbled into? Never a word was said, but something inside me warned that Mum must never be told.

# 4
# THE SCOTTISH COUSINS

*D*offie had diligently overprotected me from becoming lost or stolen while travelling about London for all of five months when, without any apparent qualms, she sent me off alone to Roxburghshire, a nine-hour and three-changes train journey, to spend the Easter holidays with Mum's Scottish cousins.

Wearing the comfortable but ugly brown leggings Doffie had bought for me, the same green dress, brown hat, tweed coat and brown shoes that I'd travelled to England in, I walked beside her down King's Cross Station platform at nine in the morning. I carried the larger of my two brown suitcases and a package of lunch. When the number on the carriage beside us matched the number on the ticket tucked inside my glove, we kissed goodbye and I boarded the London, Midland and Scottish train about to leave the station. My instructions were to change at Newark, again at Leeds and yet again at Carlisle. I was to leave the train at Hawick where I should be met at six thirty-five that evening.

Usually shy but not unfriendly, I quickly read on the icy-cold faces of my fellow travellers that it was *not done* to get chatty on a British train. The other passengers all had newspapers or books—one lady read and knitted at the same time—to keep them occupied. Since the window seats were taken, I had to look across people from the middle of a long bench to peer through the only window.

Once out of the grimy station, past signal boxes, warehouses, office buildings and thousands of small brick houses, the train picked up speed. It rattled under bridges and over bridges, through small stations without slowing up, through endless cuts and semi-tunnels and past more buildings and sudden trains coming at us that blasted the ears as they passed. Gradually fields replaced schoolyards, and villages gave way to wooded countryside. Fairly mesmerized, I simply stared and stared.

Becoming oppressed by the awful silence within the compartment, I began to experience anxiety. The thought of changing trains suddenly worried me. The possibility of getting lost became real. What if there should be no one to meet me?

Since I did not own a watch, my calculation of time had to be guesswork. Opening my little purse, where I had secured my ticket, I dug for a list of major stations Doffie and I had made so that I could gauge how far I had travelled. Just then, the conductor rolled open the door from the passage side. Breaking the silence in the compartment, he demanded to see our tickets. Being first to offer mine, I ventured to ask how long it would be till we reached Newark where I must change to another train.

"Another two hours to Newark," he answered brusquely.

"Thank you," I said. "Would you be so kind as to tell me what time it is now?" Already I had picked up the marbles-in-the-mouth, never-use-one-word-if-you-can-use-six technique.

"Ten fifteen, Miss."

I lapsed into silence again.

When I got off at Newark, I had to ask strangers which way to go and on which side of the platform I should stand to wait for my next train. After that first change I ate my sandwiches which probably wasn't wise of me because then I had absolutely nothing to look forward to.

I didn't find the scenery exciting, not like going through the Rockies, but as we travelled further north it became more interesting. Small, many-coloured fields, meticulously marked off by trimmed hedges, covered miles and miles of low, rolling hills. Here and there, copses of evergreens gave way to patches of deciduous trees filled with rookeries.

To me, rooks looked just like crows, but I had already learned that rookeries are where rooks nest—by the dozens in every tree—in all the trees in a particular patch. After the leaves have fallen, these rookeries are visible for miles. As we rode on, the living dividers gave way to neat stone walls, and the fields changed from dark earth and bright green tones to the paler, but warmer, colours of sand.

Having successfully navigated the change at Newark, I was less afraid to ask directions and found the second change, at Leeds, was easier. By the third change at the English border town of Carlisle, I knew how to follow the signs. During this last leg of my journey northeast into the Scottish lowlands, I also managed to claim a window seat from which to watch for Hawick station. By now it was growing dusk. I wondered who would come to collect me.

The only person I remembered meeting before from that part of the family was Cousin Shum, who had visited her Canadian relatives one summer and stayed at our Pasley Island cottage.

"Of course," I cheered myself, "Cousin Shum will meet me at Hawick."

I never thought of Shum as artistic, but I remember her sitting on the broad veranda steps sketching boats at anchor in Pasley's North Bay. She seemed bewildered that Mum did the cooking; she had never before seen a double-boiler. After she had gone home to Scotland, I recall that people laughed, saying she couldn't heat water! The truth is, she probably never had heated water, but she was kind, and I liked her.

I saw no one on the Hawick platform as the train arrived. My feeling of happy anticipation left me, but as I unlatched the door and clambered out of the compartment clutching my suitcase, I could see a little station house across another set of tracks.

Shum must be in the waiting room, I thought optimistically as I closed the heavy carriage door behind me. With the train pulling away beside me, I walked back a few paces and climbed metal steps to a bridge that crossed the tracks. Descending onto the other platform, I was startled when a man, dressed in a dark uniform with silver buttons, stepped out of the shadows and into my path, tipping his cap to me. I stopped.

"Are you?. . . are you. . . ?" I stammered.

"Yes M'ss. I'm Harry, M'ss. I'll carry your case. Come this way, M'ss."

Without another word between us, he took my suitcase and led the way through a gate beside the station house. I followed him across a small yard to where, against a hedge, a large, pale yellow car was parked. Harry placed my suitcase beside it and opened a back door. From the seat inside he withdrew a folded fur rug which he placed over his left arm, then he offered his gloved right hand to help me up a rather high step into the car's cream-coloured interior. When I was seated, he covered my knees with the fur rug and closed the door.

Looking about while he placed my suitcase in the luggage compartment, I discovered that there was a solid piece of glass between the driver's seat and me. Without a glance at me, Harry took his place at the wheel and started the engine which purred ever so softly. Then we drove off— away from Hawick station, through the town of Hawick and out into the country. Harry took me along narrow roads with hedges and trees high above us, between rolling hills and flat fields, through several villages with shops, and past cottages with gardens. We travelled along the side of a hill and down through a forest, all of which was charming to see. But where, I wondered, were we going? As the light faded, Harry just kept driving.

Maybe thirty or forty minutes passed, but to me it felt like hours. I had begun to dream up frightening stories about where Harry might be taking me—worrying how I might escape and find my way back to Doffie—when he increased my anxiety by turning left through huge iron gates next to a watchman's stone cottage. We drove on for several minutes, past a row of cottages opposite a long brick wall, and up a wide avenue of trees. At the top of a rise we came out of the trees and, looking down over a field with sheep in it, I could faintly discern a river. On a high bank on our side of the river sat a large, grey mansion which the car slowly approached. At last Harry pulled up under a portico beside an archway with double doors. He left me in the car while he walked to the doors and pulled the bell, then returned to stand by the car until lights came on and one of the big doors

*Makerstoun House on the River Tweed, Roxburghshire, Scotland, the home of J.J. Bell-Irving, as it appeared in the 1930s.*

opened. A second man in uniform appeared, followed by a small golden cocker spaniel. Harry opened my door and removed the rug. The dog leapt into the car and jumped up at me. At last a friend who was happy to see me!

"He's called Spen, M'ss," said Harry as he went to retrieve my suitcase.

"Hello, Spen, hello," I said, petting him.

"Good evening, Miss," said the second man. "I'm Bell, the butler. Come with me." He helped me from the car.

With nothing to carry and not knowing where to look, I scrunched down over the little dog and mumbled, "Good evening." Then, still bent over with my fingers entwined in Spen's curls, I obediently followed Bell through the open door into a huge, darkly panelled entrance hall where Spen left me. When at last I straightened up, I saw a glowing fireplace and a high arrangement of fresh flowers on a table beside it.

Halfway down the grand, curving staircase on my left stood a tall woman. Her deep voice was familiar. "Verity, my dear, do come along up. You had a pleasant journey, I trust? Harry has given your luggage to John." I turned to look for the mysterious John, but the hall was empty. Even Bell had vanished.

"How do you do, Cousin Shum?" I said, holding out my hand as I climbed up to her. She shook it robustly, and turning, led me to the top of the staircase. From thence we turned

*Verity's pen and ink drawing of her bedroom at Makerstoun House as it looked in 1934. The four-poster made her feel like the princess in the old faerie-tale "The Princess and the Pea."*

right along a balcony that crossed above the hall, right again to the end of a narrow gallery leading into a dark alcove with two doors.

"This is to be your bedroom," said Shum, opening the door to the room on the left. "Bertha will show you the bathroom when she brings your supper."

"Thank you," I replied, entering.

Before I could ask any questions at all, Shum said, "See you at breakfast, sleep well." And then she departed, closing the door.

Mouth open, I stood a moment before turning in a slow circle to take in the room. Dark, I thought, and heavy and old and silent and lonely. The room was dominated by the bed—a construction with carved wood posts holding up a ceiling of its own from which hung thick curtains with tiebacks and tassels. The mattress was so high above the floor that a small staircase had been attached to the bed frame. At the end of the bed stood my suitcase, which had already arrived by some kind of magic. A fire glowing in a small grate told me I was expected. Taking off my coat and hat, I put them over a chair by the fire.

Just then came a knock at the door, not very loud, but it was a thick door. "Come in," I called.

The door opened and in stepped a girl hardly older than myself, carrying a large wooden tray. On it was a collection of silver-looking jugs and containers, blue china dishes, cutlery, napkin and a tiny posy of flowers. She placed the tray carefully on a small table by the fire before introducing herself.

"I'm Bertha, the second housemaid."

"Hello. Thank you for bringing my suitcase up."

"Oh, I didn't, Miss. It's John as brings the luggage to the bedrooms, Miss. And ye'd be Mistress Verity?" Her voice had a lilt that I didn't recognize, but it delighted me. "I do hope your journey was not too tiresome. It's a long way to come from London in one day. I'll be closing your shutters and your curtains now and bringing warm water for your hands and face after a bit."

"Thank you, thank you so much." I was taken aback to be suddenly cared for, feeling like Cinderella when the coach arrived. "Could you. . . would you please show me where the bathroom is?"

"A' course, Miss. Come with me. Ye'll soon find your way about." She led me straight ahead along the gallery, turned right through a green baize swing door, down the corridor to the right to the last door on the left. It was an enormous, echoing room, empty but for a w.c. and a large white tub that, unlike tubs I was used to, was not on legs but set in a box. Along the wall stood towel rails made of hot-water pipes, but there were no towels.

When I got back to the room, the lamps were on and the shutters closed. Bertha had already unpacked my few belongings into a large, dark wardrobe. In the hand basin on the washstand was a polished brass hot-water jug. Linen hand towels had appeared on the rail. My dressing gown lay on the bed and Bertha was up on the step with my pyjamas over her shoulder, turning back the bedclothes.

"What will ye be wearing in the morning, Miss? Is there somethin' ye'll be wanting me to iron? "

I was totally flustered and could only mumble, "Thank you, no. Thank you."

"If ye'll put your shoes aside the door, I'll see John cleans them."

*Some members of the household staff at Makerstoun House*
*including Harry Hogg, the chauffeur (second from left, standing);*
*Bell, the butler (right standing); and John, the footman (seated). c.1940.*

"Oh, thank you."

"I'll be leaving now. It's Nan will bring the tea in the morning. Good night, Miss." Bertha disappeared, closing the door silently behind her.

Was I in faerie land? Was this a castle? Could there be dungeons down below? And what had Bertha brought me to eat? I was famished. One after the other I removed the lids of the containers and smelled the steaming contents. Soup, scrambled eggs with sausages, bread and butter and a tart. I looked for a glass of milk, but there was only a pot of tea. More than anything, I wanted something to quench my thirst, and though the tea was rather black, I drank a cupful anyway, with all the cream in it.

By the time I had finished every last morsel, I was enjoying the feeling of being a grand lady. I made a ceremony of washing my hands in the washbasin and delicately drying them on the linen towel. Having no idea what the time was, but conscious no one expected to see me before morning, I changed into night clothes and tiptoed out to find the bathroom again. I knocked, but so quietly that I thought I should knock again and since no one answered I entered. Yes, this was the right place. I hoped I wouldn't waken anyone with the loud flushing of the loo.

Back in my room I turned off all the lamps. In the light from the fire I removed my dressing gown and placed it at the foot of the bed. I approached the steps as if I were the heroine in the story of the princess and the pea, mounted them elegantly and plunged myself down into a heavenly soft sleeping place where my toes found a bed warmer. Such comfort! Such spoiling! In the moment before falling asleep, I watched the fire's gentle gold flickering on the walls and on the bed curtain.

Next morning, long before Nan knocked and entered my room carrying a bucket and jug, the bleat of sheep and their lambs had wakened me. She pulled back the curtains and opened the shutters.

"Good morning, Miss," she said, laughing as I sat up. "'Twill be another lovely day to be sure." Now this was a true Scot's voice.

"Good morning to you, too. Are you Nan?"

"Yes, Miss, and ye'll be Mistress Verity now, won't ye?"

Nan was grown-up, but she, too, seemed pleased that I had come. She took my supper tray away before bringing in a smaller tray with tea and lemon rings. Next she emptied the washbasin into a slop-bucket, wiping the basin dry before exchanging last evening's water jug for another, already filled with hot water, and replacing the linen hand towel. She opened the door of the washstand, where I could now see there was a chamber pot.

"Oh!" she said. "Ye don't need to go all the way to the bathroom in the night, Miss. I'll always empty the chamber for ye."

Was there nothing I should do for myself? "Thank you." It seemed I was always saying thank-you. "I really don't mind going to the bathroom."

"Shall I draw yer bath shortly? Or d'ye prefer it in the evening?"

I just didn't know what to say. I really wanted Nan to go away so that I could think how to start the day. "In the evening, thank you," I said at last. Again I was famished and my hunger insisted I hurry dressing and find where breakfast was. So I said thank you once again, and climbing down from my bed, went searching in the wardrobe for the skirt and jumper I had brought.

"Will ye be needing anything else, Miss?"

I couldn't think of anything except, "Where shall I find Cousin Shum?"

"She'll be having her breakfast in the dining room."

"Then there is something you can do for me and that's show me where the dining room is, please."

"That's easy," said Nan, "ye can see the door from here. Come, I'll show ye." She opened my door and pointed, first along the gallery, then the balcony. "Just follow the bannister 'round to the top of the stairs. That door standing open is where ye'll find Miss Shum."

As she left, I yet again thanked Nan, and having completely forgotten to wash, got on with dressing.

Makerstoun was the name of this house on the River Tweed near the east coast of Scotland. It belonged to my aging and distant Bell-Irving cousins, James Jardine Bell-Irving, known as J.J., and his wife, Eva Gertrude, known as Djan (pronounced Jan). They had two daughters, Ethel Mary, known as Ivy, and Eva Margaretta, known as Marda. Cousin Shum was the daughter of J.J.'s deceased brother John, and she had actually been christened Bella. She and her brother and sister—John and Elsie—had homes in Dumfriesshire near the west coast. It was Shum who had invited me to join her at Makerstoun where all the families gathered for holidays each year.

J.J. and his eight siblings had been first cousins to my Canadian grandfather, H.O. Bell-Irving, which made Shum, Elsie, John, Marda and Ivy—those with whom I became most familiar—my mother's second cousins. Marda, whose husband was Maurice Ormrod, was expected to arrive from Wales next day with her children. I found it ridiculous how often the same hereditary names were used for male children, and I couldn't believe how many Johns and Jameses collected around Djan and J.J.. When Marda brought her family—which included Oliver, Maureen and the twins, James and John, there were three Jameses and three Johns at Makerstoun. Also in the Ormrod entourage was the children's nurse, Doris Hackett, known only as Da, who quickly showed herself to be a friend to all children. And there were the Ormrod ponies.

If I hadn't been so hungry that first morning at Makerstoun, I might have felt less confident about entering the formidable dining chamber, but I could see food on a sideboard and hear Shum's voice, loud and clear. "When is J.J. going to get wise about those rabbits? Half his pet sheep are lame."

I stepped inside. "Good morning, Cousin Shum!" I heard myself say rather loudly, like Doffie. "What a comfortable bed I had last night."

Shum welcomed me and introduced me to a girl called Grizel Stuart who said she was also my cousin, and to Benjamin Piercy, just home from Italy. Grizel was a grand-daughter of J.J.'s sister and Ben was related to Djan. I joined them where they stood near one of the large windows, drinking coffee in a most unusual way. Before filling their tiny bowl-shaped cups with strong black coffee, they had piled crystals of sugar, looking like chips of amber, in their saucers. Having scooped a spoonful of amber crystals, they gently lowered it beneath the surface of the black brew, then sucked the syrupy coffee through the sugar. I quickly learned that trick.

Windows ran the whole length of the dining room, which measured close to forty feet. Shum pointed through one window at something in the "home field" that looked like a pile of huge white mushrooms. "See those, Verity?" said Shum in her loud voice. "They're rabbits. They're all J.J.'s silly rabbits. He didn't like the natural brown ones so he sowed white rabbits. Now there are hundreds of them and they burrow." I looked in amazement and started to count them. "Most of the animals on this place have broken legs, even one of his prize Belted Galloways. It's simply not safe to hold a hunt here. Too many holes!"

Finished their coffee, Grizel and Ben had returned to the sideboard to help themselves to porridge. One could also have kedgeree, scrambled eggs, boil-your-own-eggs, mixed grill (lamb chops, sausage, kidney and mushrooms) or salmon on toast, and there was cafe-au-lait and a choice of preserves.

Shum told me to help myself to anything I'd like, so when I reached for some of the luxurious fruit overflowing from several pedestalled dishes on the dining table, I was embarrassed when she said, "No, no! They're not for eating. They are some of J.J.'s prize entries from the Jedburgh exhibition. Only for show, you know! If you want fruit, take it from the sideboard."

The dining table was set for at least ten people, but only the four of us had turned up so far. I gathered that J.J. and Djan stayed in their separate apartments for breakfast. Who else, I wondered, would come to enjoy all this food?

"Would you like to take a walk over to the stables, Verity? Cunningham will be preparing loose-boxes for the Ormrod ponies." The very mention of ponies excited me. "They should arrive on the same train as the family this afternoon." Then she said, "After that we could stop in to see Djan's garden." I was all for this programme of events, but Shum changed her mind. "First," she said, "I should take you to meet Djan."

"What should I call her?" I asked as we walked toward Djan's apartment after breakfast.

"Call her Djan. Everybody does. She likes it. J.J. hates to be called Mr. Bell-Irving by anyone but a servant. But that's different." Having knocked loudly, Shum left me at Djan's door.

Nelly Jenner, Djan's private secretary-cum-head housekeeper showed me into Djan's boudoir. Remembering that Grizel had spoken of her as Aunt Eva, I held out my hand politely saying, "Good morning, Cousin Eva. How kind of you to have me."

A small, gentle-looking, grey-haired lady, dressed in an elegant though well-worn housecoat, took my hand in both of hers and led me to a little slipcovered chair by the glowing hearth.

"Sit down, my dear. Shum said you were coming. Tell me, have they looked after you? Did you sleep well?"

"Oh yes, thank you, Cousin Eva. I've just had the most scrumptious breakfast and Cousin Shum has promised to show me your garden."

"You like flowers? That's a good beginning. I'll ask Harry to take us there if you can wait a little while."

"How kind of you. Are the flowers in the entrance hall from your garden? They are lovely."

"Yes, Verity. How observant of you. Did Shum tell you that Marda is bringing her children today?"

"She did. And she said they will be bringing their ponies. I can hardly wait."

We chatted a little longer before I was ushered out with the reminder that we would later visit the walled garden.

Djan was said to be politically wise and to more or less run the county of Roxburghshire. I now suspect that the description meant she made sure the gentry kept their fishing rights and shooting coverts and maintained the various packs of hounds ad infinitum. Djan's sister, Ethel, was also influential since she had married Sir Robert "Jock" Jardine, which made her Lady Jardine. Cousin Ethel called me "Squirrel." I really liked her.

As we got to know each other, Djan realized that she had a willing helper for small chores like feeding her pet turkeys and taking Spen, her spaniel, for walks. She was pleased when she discovered how much I liked flowers and took me many times to her precious garden where she and her gardeners produced the finest delphiniums and phlox that I had ever seen. If it was my politeness that caused Cousin Eva's generosity, I was going to keep it up at all costs, for to be given free range to pick flowers in her garden and to arrange that huge bouquet in the entrance hall were two of the priceless gifts that over time she bestowed upon me.

When the Ormrod family arrived (all except father Maurice), the children seemed to accept me naturally, and I felt perfectly comfortable with them. Maureen was only six, but Oliver was my age. The twins, James and John, were just two, but since Da came with them, they were not a nuisance. Cousin Marda said she remembered my mother fondly and made me her friend and confidante from the beginning. Perhaps it had something to do with my being Canadian and her envying us our freedom from traditional behaviour. The first thing she shared with me was the rocky state of her relationship with her "shell-shocked" husband whom most of the Bell-Irving family referred to as "Poop." Probably because everyone was so rude to him there, Maurice wouldn't come to Makerstoun.

Once they had settled in, I accompanied Oliver and Maureen to the stable where I met his "Dolly Grey" and her "Tootles" as well as an old, old Shetland who was the other ponies' travelling companion. Maureen, who told me she'd rather I called her Teen, said that she could still ride the Shetland but that I was too big. And Tootles, they agreed, would be too much of a handful for a non-rider like me. Olly, however, said he would let me ride Dolly Grey in the morning because she was as safe as any rocking horse—an astute description.

When I asked where the foul smell was coming from, he told me that the hounds lived in kennels next door to the stable.

"What hounds?" I asked.

"Foxhounds, silly. Want to see them?" Without waiting for my answer, we trooped out of the stables, across the cobbled yard, through a gate and across another yard where Olly opened a door into the worst stink I can remember.

"Pew!" I said, holding my nose.

"You'll get used to it," shrugged Olly. "They eat rotting meat."

We stood between two immense cages, and there they were, dozens of big white dogs with large patches of golden-brown and black splashed all over them. They had been sleeping after their breakfast, I suppose, but when we came in they all got up and crowded to the wires to get near us. They had big jowls and floppy ears and skinny white tails that waved high above their backs. All their red tongues hung out. Suddenly one of them let out a yelp and every last hound joined in howling, "giving tongue" like nothing else on earth but foxhounds.

It frightened me a bit, but Olly and Teen obviously loved the noise and, putting their own noses in the air, added to the din until Olly yelled, "Shut up!" Amazingly, they did. It was clear these two knew about hounds and how to control them.

Despite the difference in their ages, this brother and sister got along well during the short periods when Olly was home from his boarding school, Wellington. They were equally at ease with animals, but I soon learned that they allowed their own to display terribly bad manners. Neither of their ponies would go anywhere without the other, and if one did leave, the other kicked up such a fuss, whinnying and jumping about, that they were not appreciated one bit in the hunting field.

Our Easter holidays at Makerstoun lasted two weeks, giving us ample time to get acquainted, and Olly and I became good pals. (Almost everyone else called him "Ow" because his three names began with the letter O—Oliver Ogle Ormrod.) A ruder lad I could not have imagined, but for some reason his rudeness never offended me. "Go to bed!" and "Go to hell!" were his regular put-downs. The grown-ups left us alone to go wherever we wished. All the land as far as we could walk or bicycle or ride belonged to J.J., so we could cycle from one of his stocked farms to another. Apart from falling off our bikes while full-tilting down steep, rough roads, we never got into trouble. Sometimes we'd be away half a day or more. No one seemed to care. We returned when hungry. If we were too late for a formal meal, we went to the kitchens.

When Olly was off with the *gillie*, Teen took me to the River Tweed to show me the rabbit warrens along the banks. One of the caves we walked into must have had fifteen or more rabbit doorways leading from it. Teen was also the one who first took me through the green baize doors into that different kind of rabbit warren of servant's quarters where her friends the butler, footmen, cook, several kitchen maids, scullery maid and dairy maid all worked. And Teen showed me the dumb-waiter in which all dishes and food went up or down by ropes and pulleys between the ground and nursery floors. From behind the green baize doors on the second floor, the footmen, John and James, trollied the meals from the dumb-waiter to the dining room, setting up breakfast and serving the Bell-Irving family and their guests at luncheon and dinner times.

We also visited the laundry, one of the buildings I had seen when Harry had driven me past the gate house. The laundresses showed us all the old starching and frilling irons, some of which were still in use to crisp the maids' caps and aprons. We were shown how to fold sheets outside-in, towels in three folds and many other things I remember and do to this day.

J.J. Bell-Irving, the master of all this opulence, who was 78 when I met him, gave me the feeling he had always been retired. Such a cheery, uncomplicated soul, he was rather small, slightly rotund and a bit pompous. His white hair was short and fluffy, and twinkling blue eyes peered over spectacles that perched halfway down his unaristocratic nose. His bristly moustache, which stopped at the creases of his rosy cheeks, regularly acted as a strainer for delicacies entering his eager mouth. More often than not his dress shirt, worn every evening for dinner, held in its folds evidence of misadventure from previous evenings.

On that first visit I seldom saw Djan except at teatime in the drawing room, and saw J.J. even less. But J.J. loved children with whom he was generous but whom he teased unmercifully. He himself seemed a bit childish. When he showed up for lunch or tea in the drawing or sun room, he would banter with us children and chide us for gobbling. If at lunch he surreptitiously put his hand flat on the table beside him, we youngsters knew there was some money hidden under it. We'd leave our places and gather around him to be the quickest to cover whatever it was when he raised his hand. Sometimes he'd slap his hand over the money again—as much as a pound—saying, "Too bad. Not fast enough!" and put it away in his pocket. But not always.

There were to be many more memorable holidays at Makerstoun, and I was soon hooked and fell for their whole life style. Looking back, I realize what a toffee-nosed bunch of snobs influenced my youth. It didn't take me many visits to Scotland and later Wales to learn a lot of old traditions such as who has the right to speak to whom, how people should be properly addressed, what one should wear for every occasion, how large a tip one should leave in the empty top drawer for the housemaid, how to be rude, two-faced and cruel, and how to behave like a sex-starved twit and get away with it. Did I write my mother these confusing discoveries? No, decidedly not.

# THE BELL-IRVING FAMILY
## OF SCOTLAND AND WALES

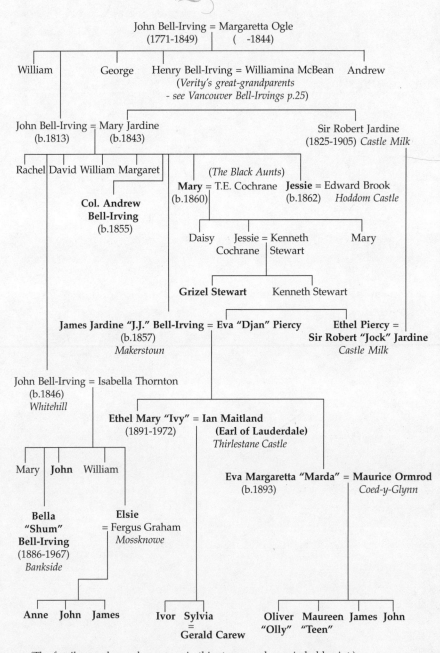

John Bell-Irving = Margaretta Ogle
(1771-1849)     (    -1844)

William     George     Henry Bell-Irving = Williamina McBean     Andrew
(*Verity's great-grandparents*
*- see Vancouver Bell-Irvings p.25*)

John Bell-Irving = Mary Jardine     Sir Robert Jardine
(b.1813)     (b.1843)     (1825-1905) *Castle Milk*

Rachel David William Margaret

**Col. Andrew
Bell-Irving**
(b.1855)

(*The Black Aunts*)
**Mary** = T.E. Cochrane     **Jessie** = Edward Brook
(b.1860)     (b.1862)     *Hoddom Castle*

Daisy     Jessie = Kenneth     Mary
Cochrane   Stewart

**Grizel Stewart**     Kenneth Stewart

**James Jardine "J.J." Bell-Irving** = Eva "Djan" Piercy     **Ethel Piercy** =
(b.1857)     **Sir Robert "Jock" Jardine**
*Makerstoun*     *Castle Milk*

John Bell-Irving = Isabella Thornton
(b.1846)
*Whitehill*

**Ethel Mary "Ivy"** = Ian Maitland
(1891-1972)     **(Earl of Lauderdale)**
*Thirlestane Castle*

Mary    **John**    William

**Eva Margaretta "Marda"** = Maurice Ormrod
(b.1893)     *Coed-y-Glynn*

**Bella
"Shum"
Bell-Irving**
(1886-1967)
*Bankside*

**Elsie**
= Fergus Graham
*Mossknowe*

**Anne John James**     **Ivor Sylvia**     **Oliver Maureen James John**
                =
              **Gerald Carew**     **"Olly" "Teen"**

(The family members who appear in this story are shown in bold print.)

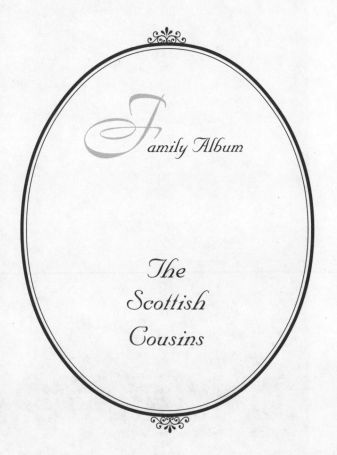

*Family Album*

*The
Scottish
Cousins*

*Thirlestane Castle overlooking Leader Water, 28 miles southeast of Edinburgh. View from the park, showing front entrance and four towers.*

Inset: Portrait of Mrs. J.J. "Djan" Bell-Irving flanked by her daughters.
Ethel Mary (Ivy), left, and Eva Margaretta (Marda), right. c. 1900.

James Jardine "J.J." Bell-Irving with Maureen Ormrod and her
twin brothers in the summer house at Makerstoun. 1935.

Left: Verity Sweeny, age 12, at
Makerstoun House. The children
are the Ormrod twins. 1934.

Below: Mrs J.J. "Djan" Bell-Irving
with her grandchildren, Oliver,
Maureen, James and John at their
home, Coed-y-Glynn, in Wrexham,
Wales. c. 1936.

Bella "Shum" Bell-Irving of Bankside, fishing at Glencalvie on the River Carron in 1922. Aged 36.

Left: Shum Bell-Irving riding sidesaddle on Grey Dawn at a fox hunting meet at Clughead, near Annan, Dumfries, November 11, 1929.

Below: Photo from **The Illustrated Sporting and Dramatic News,** November 1, 1919. Mrs. J. Bell-Irving, Mr. John Bell-Irving Jr., Mr. J. Bell-Irving Sen., Miss Bell-Irving and Col. A. Bell-Irving.

*Shum Bell-Irving and her brother John Bell-Irving of "Whitehill" near Annan, Dumfries, Scotland, at the Jedburgh Horse Trials in 1932.*

*Three brothers Bell-Irving at dog trials. From Left, David Jardine, James Jardine and John.*

*Above: The Hunt Coming up Towards Webber's Post, with the Somerset staghounds, 1930.*

*Grizel Stewart, Verity Sweeny and Anne Graham at a picnic outside the ruin of Milkbank near Lockerbie, Dumfries, Scotland. 1934.*

Verity picking daffodils at
Rycott, the home of the
Hamersleys. Aged 12.

Anne Graham
and Verity about to swim in
the Water O' Milk.

Oliver "Olly" Ormrod at Makerstoun. 1935.

*Verity on the bank of the River Tweed near Makerstoun House.*
*Aged 13. 1935.*

*Above: Verity at Makerstoun House on Dolly Grey with Maureen "Teen" Ormrod on Tootles. 1935.*

*Below: Verity riding Batie with her brother Malcolm on Lucy Grey. 1935.*

*JB of Milkbank discusses "the hunt," early 1920's.*

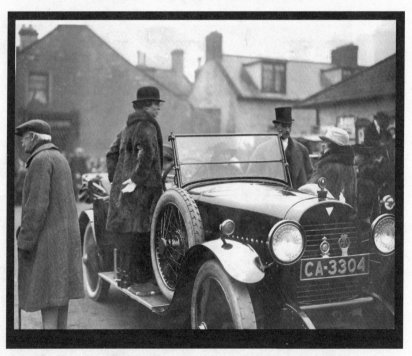

*Shum's 1922 finery, as she converses from the running board,*
*included a Canadian sealskin coat, a stylish bowler and light kid gloves.*

*Lady Sylvia Maitland riding astride on Blue Bird with her mother.*
*the 15th Countess of Lauderdale, Ivy Maitland (nee Bell-Irving)*
*riding sidesaddle on the matched grey, Two O'clock. c. 1937.*

*Whitehill, the home of John and Isabella Bell-Irving*

*Bankside, the home of Bella "Shum" Bell-Irving*

*Makerstoun House above the River Tweed. In the foreground,*
*Grizel Stewart and her aunt, Mrs. J.J. "Djan" Bell Irving. c. 1938.*

*Verity photographed by Aunt Doffie's friend,*
*Audrey Estob, in Chelsea, London. 1936.*

# 5
# THE SOCIAL WHIRL

*D*offie met me at King's Cross on my return from Scotland. We taxied home to a very different atmosphere at Cheyne Cottage. While I had been in Scotland, the Duff-Arnotts had left. I believe Doffie sponsored them on a trip to see what they could find in Hollywood, but I don't know where the dogs went.

During my first months in England, Doffie had taken me to see—among other things—a massed symphony concert at the Albert Hall, Russian ballet at Covent Garden and the changing of the guard at Buckingham Palace. When June came, it was time for my next adventure which, I was told, would be much bigger and more exciting than any of those. My governess was to take me to the annual celebration of the signing of the Magna Carta at Runnymede. The tickets had been on the hall shelf for several weeks.

The night before the event, Doffrey and Aunt Doffie had been up late with their friends, and as usual, because of their laughing and singing, I had been kept awake. When at last they had gone to bed, Aunty's coughing kept everyone awake.

I had taken breakfast to the upstairs lot—toast, coffee and carefully cut, sugared grapefruit—but they had all been asleep and weren't happy to see me or it. I had eaten my own grapefruit—how I loathed that bitter taste—and toast, and was as prepared as I knew how to be.

At ten o'clock, gloves in hand, I was waiting by the front door. When Miss Richardson arrived at eleven, she said she was sorry to be late, but if we hurried, we could still make it to Runnymede by two o'clock, the time of the performance.

"Come, Verity, we'll catch a bus on the King's Road. Hurry!" I expected her to run through those crooked streets, but sadly, Miss Richardson herself didn't know what hurry meant. When we got to the King's Road, a long queue was already waiting for the Number 19 bus which ran every ten minutes. But two full busses passed without stopping. Finally we squeezed onto the third.

"Seating upstairs only, Miss," said the conductor. So up we climbed on the spiral treads. At Waterloo train station we found our way to the appropriate wicket but had to queue again for tickets. We set off for platform six. Oh how I wished Miss Richardson could run! We must have just missed a train because when we got there the platform was empty. Having changed at Clapham Junction, we waited again at Wimbledon to struggle into a packed carriage. The final bus from Runnymede station went nowhere near the grandstand, but the crowds were still filing in when, after walking as fast as we could, we reached our entrance-way. Together Miss Richardson and I climbed almost to the roof of the immense grandstand.

Finding our seats, three in from the aisle, we were no sooner seated and peering down at the scene of tents and fluttering flags on the greensward below than trumpets declared the pageant had begun. From out of the woods on left and right with pomp and splendour came troops of horses wearing armour and draped in ceremonial cloaks. Their riders were helmeted and plumed and their chain mail glinted in the sun as these soldiers from opposing camps jogged dramatically toward each other across this famous island in the River Thames. With lances raised in salute, they halted, face to face.

I felt more excitement than I could bear. Without warning, I vomited my bitter breakfast all over the man sitting in front of me and was dragged away sobbing by two St. John's Ambulance men. With one on each side, my arms held in a strong grip, they hurried me down steep back stairs to lay me upon a stretcher in a shadeless grassy field. Miss Richardson followed us down but soon went back to see the show. With nothing in my stomach, I continued to retch helplessly every few minutes most of the afternoon, overwhelmed by the still-vivid memory of lying seasick in my deckchair during the hurricane.

My next letter to Mum at home in Vancouver read:

*Darling Mummy,*
*Yesterday Miss Richardson took me to Runnymede.*
*It was very exciting. There were lots of horses. Our seats*
*were up very high on a grandstand looking down on a sort*
*of park where the Thames has an island and there were*
*trees instead of scenery. The horses were dressed up with a*
*lot of armour and harness that jingled and feathers and*
*silk sheets that almost covered them, and the men wore*
*silver. There were trumpets and lots of people shouted. I*
*think of you all, all the time.*

Since my parents could do nothing to change things, I felt it my responsibility not to inflict the whole truth on them.

One Sunday, Aunty Doffie and Doffrey surprised me by being up early. They said we were going to church, which was a further surprise. Not only that, we were going to Westminster Abbey where coronations and royal weddings took place. Even I knew a few things about Westminster Abbey and it made me feel solemn and grand to be going there.

Although Doffrey didn't bother about covering her head, Doffie wore her mannish brown felt hat. Of course, I wore my hat and gloves, and I put my small prayer book in the pocket of my tweed coat. Off we walked toward the embankment where my aunt put two fingers between her lips and whistled loudly to hail a taxi. It quickly appeared around the corner from Oakley Street.

When there were three of us, I always sat on the pull-down seat. We drove all along the embankment, and since it was a bright day I had a wonderful view looking back at the barges and boats on the river. I wasn't the least interested in their conversation, which ranged from Miss Partridge, the landlady, to the behaviour of their friends. Having heard a record of the choir and seen pictures of royal ceremonies there, I was far away, imagining the Abbey.

Suddenly Doffrey said, "Turn around, Verity. You're missing the view."

Indeed I was, because when I twisted and looked ahead, the sun was bright on the buildings across the Thames and a bristle of church spires on our side looked like solid gold. I sucked in my breath. "Is one of those the Abbey?"

We were early for the service and to my delight, could take our time looking at the Abbey from the outside before we slowly entered it. Westminster Abbey was cavernous and though hundreds of people were already inside, it seemed quiet. Speaking softly, Doffrey and Aunt Doffie decided where we should sit. Doffrey went in first, me next, then with Aunty making a clatter as she hooked her stick on the pew in front, we slid past a few people to put ourselves near the middle. While the two women chattered, I sat down, lowered my head and closed my eyes just for a moment. When I looked up again I began to take in the details. Directly in front were the choir stalls with two carved wooden shafts rising up to join the wooden ceiling with its intricate designs. I felt the "reaching up" of the whole place and wished the women would be quiet.

The pews were filling up. Noisily, because of Aunty's stick, we slid closer together. When organ music began softly, Doffrey and Doffie were still chattering across me, but louder now because of the music, and I began to realize that I was the only one of our group who felt obliged to be quiet. My companions had only come to sightsee and their comments about the pompous carriage and ornate robes of the clergy told me they had absolutely no respect for the sanctity of the place. When the choir boys in their scarlet cassocks took their places, Doffie giggled and said in a voice loud enough for everyone in the next three pews to hear, "Look at that mother's boy! Did you ever see anything so cherubic?"

"But look over here," countered Doffrey. "That little fatty can hardly see past his ruff!"

I would have gladly melted and vanished through the old floorboards into the dark crypt. I guess I shouldn't have been surprised by Doffie's behaviour as she often poked fun at other people's beliefs. But did she have to embarrass me in public?

The two Ds and I lived in the cottage through another winter and spring, lapping up a lot of culture. Often it came to us in the form of improvised drawing room performances by a handful of Doffie's professional friends. Despite threats by phone from Miss Partridge, the landlady—whom I never actually saw—to throw us out because of the many exuberant parties, Doffie's friends came night after night, playing the piano, singing, reading, or telling bawdy stories. It was often rowdy because they drank a lot, but sometimes one of them would sing or play something beautiful and touching. In the momentary silence that would follow I could feel their emotion when for once nobody said a word.

One of Doffie's regular visitors was de Beezer, a dark-complexioned wraith whose long, bony fingers could pull magic from a keyboard. De Beezer—she had no other name—seemed immune to cold or hunger. Summer or winter she wore sandals and a shantung sheath buttoned high at the neck. From between her thin but curving lips dangled a Turkish cigarette. The only food I saw her eat was bananas, no surprise to me since all that remained of her teeth were black spikes. Her voice was sepulchral, too.

I suspect de Beezer had difficulty finding a place where her talent was appreciated. Once she appeared at the cottage with her dark hair cut like a Buddhist monk with a perfectly round bald spot at the back. She was jubilant because she had been hired by Hindu dancer Uday Shankar to play water bowls in his orchestra. I had seen the Shankar troupe and knew that the music was made by men who sat cross-legged, their backs to the audience, in a curve at the front of the stage. Every one of them showed the same bald spot. Doffie did try to help de Beezer by introducing her to my dance school. For a time this odd-looking woman turned up to play for class, but that didn't last long because de Beezer could not manage to arrive on time.

Another remarkable Chelsea pianist made frequent visits to our area with his piano-on-wheels. Moving about from one favourite place to another, he set up his piano where he knew people would listen. It was said he made a better livelihood on the street than he could in a concert hall because of the money people gave him after each half-hour concert. Once I saw Doffie give him a five pound note.

He would play out-of-doors until long after dark and the shouting had begun. "Why don't you go home?" "I need some sleep!" Or other things not so polite. Then he'd lock and cover the fine-toned instrument and enter Cheyne Cottage to play Doffie's grand piano until Miss Partridge banged on the wall between her house and ours—the wall against my cupboard.

Often, after they'd all gone to bed, I lay awake listening for sounds of the River Thames, the friendly throb of barge engines, fog horns and boat whistles. And although I never got enough sleep, morning time also had special pleasures for me because I was the early riser. There were hawkers' calls and a bell that heralded the muffin man. Sometimes Doffie would call to me to catch him as she threw on her dressing gown and went to find money to buy hot muffins or the crumpets which I preferred. And as the day wore on, there was the black-faced "cawl" man with a sack of coal over his shoulder, and the vegetable man whose waggon of tasty morsels always included specialties like potted ginger and mangoes, tree tomatoes and passion fruit. Once the man even had a basket full of kittens. Doffie got me one that I called Puss-in-Boots after the pantomime we'd just seen, but she insisted on calling him Tooten. Who knows why? I loved scratching the nose of the man's dear little pony and savoured the familiar sweet stable odour that rose, steaming, from his droppings along the curb. Then there were the flower carts. Of all Doffie's weaknesses, this was the one we shared from the start. Mimosa, wallflowers, lilies-of-the-valley, anemone, freesia and violets. Oh, the smell of violets! I was never refused if I asked for money for flowers.

In my second year with Doffie, I was allowed to stay downstairs for dinner and for an hour or so after dinner. The songs Doffie sang to her own powerful piano accompaniment were more often than not sad—"Danny Boy," "Macushla," Eriskay (Highland-Gaelic) love lilts, love songs and laments—and though she didn't actually cry, her voice cried and tears fell among her listeners. She and her friends encouraged me to sing with them all the great Coward and Cole Porter lyrics, and occasionally someone even asked me to dance a little. It was a rich and sensuous atmosphere for a young person to absorb.

One of her visitors, photographer Audrey Estob, invited

me to her studio to pose for her in dance costume. Doffie took me there and I had my picture taken in a long dress with a sheer skirt and silver shoes. But they had other things in mind. A bolt of cream-coloured silk was produced, and a drapery wrapped about my bare body. Folding it to the width of my lower back, they covered my bottom, passed it from back to front between my legs like a diaper, then pulled it up my front and threw it over my left shoulder. Then they pinned the back to the front at each side of my waist, making the front wide enough to cover my chest, and gathered up the part on my shoulder, tying it with a bit of string and leaving a length to fall behind me to the floor. This I could hold, wrap around me or walk away from. I felt that the end result was Egyptian or Greek and tried to make my body into representative shapes, but I wasn't too sure I liked doing it.

Doffie had many other friends who lived in and around Chelsea. Most of them were artists and theatre people who belonged to the famous—or perhaps infamous—Pheasantry Club that she belonged to. An endless number of its members came to Cheyne Cottage, including a grand old lady whose name was Mrs. Galsworthy, mother of the famous John. One day I was taken to tea with this lady in her London home. Within a week, I had an invitation to spend a weekend at her country estate where she planned to take her grand-daughter.

Only a couple of events remain clear from that visit. I had my first real cigarette, courtesy of Miss Galsworthy whose first name I've forgotten. Our hiding place was out of sight from the house behind gorse bushes at the bottom of a field that sloped to a lake where there were swans. I remember feeling cold and woozy afterwards.

I also recall a huge, shiny dining table in a huge, dark dining room with Mrs. Galsworthy at the teapot end, where she served a dreadful concoction she had asked Cook to make especially on account of my visit—a sort of stiff, tasteless blancmange mould that stood high and wobbly on a bare plate, its innards filled with powdered bitter chocolate. That dessert nearly choked me, but I knew better than to refuse.

Invitations also came from families I'd never heard of. One weekend, an hour south of London, I found myself watching two girls, said to be my cousins, training polo ponies. I liked their parents and I liked the food we ate, but I wasn't sure why I was there because the girls, seventeen or so years old, were entirely preoccupied with their brilliant careers as horse trainers and as the first female polo players. I was told they had even trained polo ponies for the royal family. Enchanted with riding after my small taste of it at Makerstoun, I was glad enough to be there, even just watching.

Not long after my visit to Makerstoun, I received another invitation from Cousin Shum. Having picked me up at Lockerbie station in Dumfriesshire, she drove me the fifteen miles to her home, Bankside. A squarish stone house, it sat on a bluff overlooking fields and a slow moving river, the Water O' Milk. It had comfortable charm and some no-doubt valuable paintings and antiques which Shum had come by in the natural order of inheritance. I was ignorant of all but the feel of the place, which was not nearly so small or cold as it first appeared. Out of sight behind the house were kennels, two servants' cottages, a dairy-cum-vegetable cellar and gardens. There, removed from traffic and other dwellings, I was kept awake at night by the unusual sounds of the river and forest.

Shum may have been born in China. I recall someone saying that her nickname meant "little one" in Chinese. I do know that some of my mother's Scottish relatives had made their fortunes in the Hong Kong company of Jardine Matheson, in opium, tea, oil and other exports.

When I knew her, Shum still rode to hounds sidesaddle on her huge black horse, although it was said that, long ago, she had watched her fiance fall to his death in a collision of horses going over a fence. I can't remember who said it, but the words were said in a "poor Shum" tone of voice. *Poor Shum*. I sensed that her heart had been broken and felt sad for her, but I wonder now if she wasn't one of the least poor. I never heard her criticise or complain or blame. Shum didn't gossip or judge or argue or snub like some of the Scottish family I had already met. She just was.

I loved Cousin Shum—which is the way I addressed her until, when I was about thirteen, she said I might drop the cousin part. (Although I wanted to, I found that difficult.) When I visited her at Bankside, she would treat me with importance, taking me with her wherever she had to go and planning the days so that I should not be lonely there, so far away from home.

Shum's voice was like a crow. "What, Child?" she rasped, then pressed her lips together and wiggled them from side to side. Maybe it was the whiskers that bothered her. "Yes, Child?" Perhaps she was a little deaf.

"Shall we go for another walk today?" I asked again.

"Of course, Child!" It wasn't unfriendly. With genuine excitement she and I would go out even before breakfast with Spot, her border terrier, to gather mushrooms from under the hedges, just enough for Cook to put on toast to serve the two of us in the big, dark dining room.

Shum introduced me to the Graham cousins—Fergus, Elsie and their three children—who lived about ten miles away at Mossknowe, an ancient farm near Ecclefechan, not far from the English border. The house, nearly 200 years old, was desperately cold in winter. James, John and Anne swam with me in the River Annan near their home and in the Milk near Shum's which, passing through flat fields, never seemed

*Above, Bankside in the spring of 1998.*

to rise or fall but somehow stayed colder in summer than even I could enjoy for swimming.

They also walked me from Shum's house across a little bridge over the Milk to the big house called Milkbank. Although it stood empty and the doors were locked, we could see through the windows and get glimpses of the entrance hall and corridors. My mother, speaking of her own child-hood visits, had told me she once slid from the very top of the curved banister, knocking over a great aunt as she landed at the bottom.

"Those ill-mannered Canadians!" that relative had said.

The Grahams and I picked mushrooms together and they lent me their pony. Their Mum, Cousin Elsie, treated me as one of her children. Wherever we went, there were ponies and horses because these were hunting, shooting and fishing people, and it was on these visits that I became acquainted with the real country life of Scotland.

The first time I stayed at Coed-y-Glynn, the beautiful Welsh farm where Major Maurice Ormrod and his family resided, it was abundantly obvious to me that his family were disappointed in him, but I also saw plenty of reasons why he should be disappointed in them as well. He came from a good old Welsh family in Denbighshire where he one day hoped to inherit his father's estate, Pickhill Hall near Wrexham. Rather introverted by the time I met him and somewhat sullen-looking, he was still handsome. Tall and slim with a china-white complexion, he had straight jet-black hair and dark eyes. A slightly shaggy mustache more or less obscured a sensitive, overly rosy mouth. (His son Oliver had inherited this colouring exactly.)

Once at Makerstoun I had heard it babbled that he was not faithful, that he had an eye for a pretty lady. I decided that this might be understandable. Although Marda was a free spirit with a bawdy sense of humour, she was no longer pretty. And at Coed-y-Glynn I seldom heard her address him except in criticism. "Did you have to take the last grapefruit?" or "Must you park that hulk of a Daimler right where the children ride out of the stable?" or to the children, "Poop could have been civil and spoken to your grandmother on the telephone." The children spoke rudely past their father. They even spoke about him in his presence as though he

*Part of the Bell-Irving estate, Milkbank was locked and unoccupied when Verity visited. c. 1920.*

couldn't hear. Much as I loved Marda and Olly and Teen, the twins and the rest of the retinue, I felt desperately sorry for Maurice who took their rudeness without a word and kept himself out of sight as much as possible. I wondered what they blamed him for. I couldn't guess what unpardonable sin he had committed, and except for the gossip about his roving eye, I never found out.

Coed-y-Glynn had rambling private gardens as well as stables. It had paddocks where the children rode, and hunting coverts between fields that produced hay and what we call wheat but they call corn. Maurice did some of the flower and kitchen-gardening and that's where I ran into him most often, hunched over, weeding.

My predilection for gardening gave us a good connection. Perhaps he had been shell-shocked, whatever that meant. Maybe he was a silent drinker or just didn't like people, but I liked what I saw of him and he was never unkind to me. Because I was not rude, he'd reply to my "Good morning!" with a surprised look and perhaps a mumbled, "'Morning." We even chatted a bit, and he asked me if I was interested in backgammon.

"Black gammon?" I queried. "Do you mean to eat?"

"No." He actually laughed. "It's a game I pass time with. I can play it alone or with others."

"I'll try if you wish. Where do you play it?"

"In the library, across the hall from the dining room."

"I've not been in that room."

"How about after lunch?"

"If Cousin Marda has nothing for me to do, I'll come."

And so began a simple friendship between two often lonely people. I don't know what became of him in the evenings. He disappeared after dinner and I went upstairs with Marda or to the nursery where Da cared for the twins and saw Teen into her night-dress. Olly must have been away at Wellington school. When it was time for bed, Marda filled hot-water bottles for the two of us in a maid's pantry near the bathroom. It was there that she introduced me to her fairy. "This is my special fairy," she said, pointing to a dainty figure stamped within an oval on her hot-water bottle. "I talk to my fairy every night. Fairy, I say, please take Poop away. I cannot bear to be near him." A deep sadness for them all came over me.

I think Marda one day got part of her wish. During World War II, Maurice did go away for some time, but when he eventually inherited his father's estate, he returned to Wales and moved his family to Pickhill Hall. Just a few years later, when he was busy supervising changes to Pickhill's kitchen, he suddenly looked past the workman he was speaking to, smiled and said "Oliver," then dropped dead. Olly had been lost over Malta while serving with the RAF.

On a Saturday morning late in August 1934, Doffie put me on a train to Brighton. I was to be picked up by a Mrs. Arkell who would take me to spend the weekend at her guest house in Shoreham. I never questioned Doffie's motives, but I guessed she and Doffrey had activities planned into which I didn't fit.

It was probably noon when I arrived. Several elderly visitors sat about in a stuffy drawing room that had windows looking out to sea, but no one seemed interested in going out-of-doors, let alone venturing onto the shadeless, sandy beach—creamy gold, as I remember it—stretching for miles east and west and falling quite precipitously toward the bluest of white-capped seas.

As soon as possible after a sandwich and tea I changed into my swimsuit covered by shorts. A cool breeze deceived me into believing I needed no protection from the sun. Towel in hand, I headed for a place near the water. There I shed my shorts and sandals and dashed into the waves, which quickly threw me back on shore with my mouth full of sand. Watching some youngsters further along the beach, I saw that they dove through an incoming wave and bounced up beyond it. Copying them, I found that if I jumped high enough I could avoid the heavy push and pull as the waves came and went. I jumped from a sandbar, higher and higher. What a thrill! No one warned me about the undertow which must have been what took me by surprise a few times, leaving me far out of my depth but in less rough water. I must have had a guardian angel.

Coming in for a rest, I soaked up the sun, watching salt crystals dry on my skin. My eyebrows and hair were stiff with them, and my eyes stung. Then back I went to play in the waves. I can still feel the joy of it. It must have been about four o'clock when I dragged myself away from my games. Already I felt a bit sick from swallowing salt water and from too much sun, but back at the guest house I changed from my swimsuit to shirt and shorts and went to have tea.

"Good gracious, child, you haven't half scorched yourself," said one of the ladies. "Have you seen your face?" No, I hadn't seen my face, but I could feel my whole body beginning to shrivel up. My arms and legs were getting brighter and brighter red, and I didn't feel well.

I told Mrs. Arkell, "I think I'd like to go home tonight. Can we telephone Aunty?"

"She's not expecting you, is she?"

"No, but I need to go home."

"We'll give her a call."

"No luck," said Mrs. Arkell, "she's not in. Is there someone else who could look after you?"

"Perhaps Aunty Shirley, Mrs. Radford. Could you ring her? She lives in Sloane Square." I waited while Mrs. Arkell found a London phone book and looked up Radford. Aunt Shirley and Uncle Basil were away, but Irene, the maid, after listening to the story of my plight, said I could come. Feeling decidedly shaky, I rolled my wet suit in my towel and repacked my pyjamas. "How soon can I get a train, Mrs. Arkell?

"They run every half hour. I could get you to the five o'clock."

I clearly recall sitting bolt upright on the edge of the train seat for the best part of an hour to Horsham and over an hour more to Victoria Station. My few clothes were already sticking to me and I dared not let the back of the seat touch me. My throat burned, my lips were splitting and my legs stuck straight out in front of me because my knees didn't want to bend. I had enough money to take a taxi to the Radfords' and turned up on their doorstep about to fall over.

"Come in, my dear," said Irene. "What have you done to yourself?"

"I didn't know the sun was so hot. Can I lie down on the floor where it's cool? On my tummy, my back hurts so...."

"Look, I'll put down some cushions with a sheet over them. You can rest there while I fetch a cool drink and ointment to rub on your burns. Take everything off, my poor shrimp, we'll fix you up!"

And fix me up she did. I wanted to scream when the dear lady tried to spread stiff white ointment on my back, scraping it on in big chunks, breaking blisters that had already started to rise. Oh, it hurt! I couldn't have turned over for her to do my front. Finally I fell asleep where I lay. Next day Doffie came to collect me. Once home, she put me into her bed because it was bigger than my cot. And when Doffrey came, she brought cooling lotion and insisted I drink a lot of water. By Monday I felt better, but my whole body was covered with huge blisters. On Tuesday Doffie delivered me to dance class but I really couldn't dance. I remember, several days later, Phyllis Dakin began stripping the peeling skin from my arms. It didn't hurt but it looked revolting. Redheads really should be told not to go on a beach—especially in August.

# 6
## PREPARING FOR A LIFE IN THE THEATRE

*L*uckily for me, in the era of my dance studies in England there was no emphasis on the "Perfect Body." Although I remember some enviably beautiful bodies, many of us students had difficulties to overcome such as too-square shoulders, short necks, big hands, and legs that didn't really fit our bodies. I had particularly poor turn-out and was not naturally limber, nor was my face classic. Perhaps only a few of our crowd had a ghost of a chance to succeed as dancers, but some of the least well-formed of us were the hardest workers. So long as we tried, there seemed to be hope.

Stories went around about successful dancers who had been sent to dancing school to correct knock-knees or bowed legs. Everyone knew that Markova's legs were far from straight. Fortunately, in those days, technique was subordinated to personality and artistry. Dancers were definitely looked upon as individuals who succeeded according to their command of the audience, their personal popularity.

There were no mirrors in the studios where I worked. Perhaps it was a good thing. Had I seen myself, my inferiority would have overwhelmed me. As it was, I had difficulty enough organizing my body to co-operate with the signals I sent it. Though I was supposed to look up as I surrounded my head with the fifth position of arms, my short neck meant there seemed no space between my arms and my ears, which were mighty close to my high shoulders. My legs, which were several inches too short for my body, were bumpy and curved enough to make the closed foot positions—heel in front of other toe, toe in front of other heel—virtually impossible unless my knees were flexed. For the longest struggling time I could only compromise. *Pliés* (deep knee bends) in open fourth position were horribly uncomfortable. It was years before I could throw my leg (*battement*) above hip level and even then the knee of my supporting leg twisted and its heel left the floor.

But I could spin. I could hop, skip, and spring all over the place. I ran fast and jumped high and threw myself into *grandes jetés* with fury. I loved all the children's dances—hornpipe, Irish jig and polka—and I was a natural at mime—stroke an animal that wasn't there, brush my hair without a brush, pretend to drink, to sing, to fight, to be afraid, to poke fun, to be angry or sad or happy. These sorts of things I knew how to express.

I learned to use my hands and arms by repeating smooth and gentle movements many, many times, and I finally gained control of my shoulders, leaving them relaxed and low, no matter how high my arms reached. As I became co-ordinated, I could begin to find my centre of balance by pulling opposing sets of muscles equally strongly away from centre, sideways, high to low, front to back. I felt my shoulder pull away from fingertip, hip pull away from stretched foot. A picture of each position I aimed for became clear in my head, giving me time for careful linking movements between them, each one calculated as though in slow motion. Although I couldn't watch it in a mirror, couldn't see these details in myself, I could see them and could feel them—or the lack of them—in others. I learned to feel how they moved and to transfer those feelings to my own body. This kind of criticism was a necessary learning tool. Later criticism would become competitive and often ugly, and I grew to loathe it.

Looking back, I realize how blessed I was to have studied dance in London at that time. Art in general and dance in particular was coming to a fifty-year peak all over the world and, because of the Russian Revolution, many of Russia's finest classical dancers and choreographers and teachers had settled in London. In those days huge companies—complete with sets and musicians—toured from one country to another for months on end without border restrictions. As they would stay in London for weeks at a time, we students became familiar with their repertoires and knew individual artists well enough to gauge what sort of performances they were capable of. Seats were cheap and seeing *everything* was considered valuable to our training.

What's more we, as audience, were an integral part of performances. Being informed and critical in those days, audiences responded vigorously, holding nothing—neither negative nor positive reactions—back. When the time came for us to voice our opinions we applauded honestly—long and loud when we liked what we saw and in a desultory manner if we felt they were sloppy. We used our voices, thumped the floor and called their names when we approved. And there were those wonderful times when everyone knew a performer had excelled, and a deep hush would drop upon the final gesture of their performance before anyone dared breathe "Bravo!" It was heady stuff.

Although by then I was enchanted with changing sets and moving stages, with flying Peter Pans and balletic *pirouettes*, I was even more attracted to individual performers who demonstrated a deep commitment to their art. I identified with them and avidly followed their careers. I believe I was privy to a very special banquet of flowering talent that was, in general, less commercial and more artistically honest than we see today.

During my hundreds of attendances at Sadler's Wells, Drury Lane, Covent Garden and Marie Rambert's Mercury Theatre, I witnessed the coming of age of scores of young dancers whose every mannerism, weakness and strength were my personal education. Sometimes even today in my semi-sleep, I can still catch glimpses of Jose Greco, of Ted Shawn and Barton Mumaw, of the Russian "baby ballerinas" Irina Baronova and Tamara Toumanova. In reality I saw them all many times, knew their capabilities, felt I knew them personally and followed their lead in my own work. While I was still a struggling student, I was able to observe the young Alicia Markova, Anton Dolin, Frederick Ashton, Robert Helpmann and all that crowd polishing their techniques and styles under the eye of Marie Rambert in her minute Mercury Theatre—so small that the performers had to enter and leave the stage by the centre aisle. It was a favourite place for Doffie and me, this theatre where so much new work was being created, so many stars were being born.

I was introduced to Spanish dance by La Argentina, the greatest of all Spanish dancers. Argentina—not to be confused with her follower, Argentinita—was a personality of huge dimension with a body to support it. Tall and generously built, flexible but firm as a rock, she danced with grace and a powerful fire in the most glorious of ruffled costumes of her own design. It is said that no one ever played castanets like Argentina. I can vouch for the fact that she talked with them, chatted and argued and romanced with them. A pure delight to hear, but not to be enjoyed for long. In 1936 Argentina died suddenly in Paris. I never quite forgave Argentinita, beautiful as she was, for benefiting from Argentina's name and brilliance.

This growing knowledge was in stark contrast to my utter ignorance when Doffie first took me on. One of my earliest memories of being a disappointment to her occurred when we sat at the very top of the Royal Albert Hall for a concert of massed symphony orchestras under the baton of Sir Thomas Beecham. This mind-boggling theatrical experience began in a taxi, with Doffie trying to prepare me for what lay ahead. The Royal Albert Hall, she explained, was named after Prince Albert, Queen Victoria's husband. Although a king who married a commoner could raise her to the rank of queen, a queen could not so honour her consort. Prince Albert had loved and pampered Queen Victoria—so Aunty told me and I assumed she had inside knowledge of this—but Victoria had never let him be her equal. Though her people had respected and admired her, they had come to adore Prince Albert, Doffie said.

I had already seen the tall and elegant Albert Memorial which stands just inside the railings of Kensington Gardens. It shows the two of them together under a little dome that is held up by pillars. I had been impressed with its gentleness. But the memorial is dwarfed by the great dome of the Royal Albert Hall just across Kensington Road. In the taxi Doffie had given me the statistics of size and accommodation, but all this historical and numerical detail was much more than I could take in. Unfortunately, whenever I was overwhelmed, my unconscious reaction was to sigh deeply. This did not please my aunt.

"Don't sigh like that! It's rude." Now I felt horribly small, but it was nothing compared with the smallness I was to feel as we entered Albert Hall and began the long, steep climb to its topmost rim. Doffie huffed and puffed and had to stop a few times. Emerging from the last flight of stairs, we passed through an archway to a circular gallery, climbing to our seats on the highest row. The circumference and height of the place were dizzying. I could see three gilded galleries below us with dozens of archways circling out, right and left, then many more rows of open seating. I was amazed when literally hundreds of musicians began to take their places in a giant semi-circle—two thirds of the circle of Albert Hall—close to a very small... "What's it called, Aunty?"... podium on which a conductor was to stand. Below us, thousands of people filled almost all the remaining seats in order to hear this special symphony concert.

Suddenly Doffie turned to me in something of a huff and took hold of my right hand in which I held a crumpled booklet. "Why aren't you reading the programme?"

Dutifully I opened the thing I had scrunched in my excitement. "The programme?"

"Yes, this!" She retrieved and straightened the pages. Now I had done something else wrong. "You'll never know what they play if you don't study it!" Programme? What was a programme? What should it tell me? I knew nothing of programmes. I'd never before seen an orchestra, let alone three full symphony orchestras massed under the baton of one man. Who was he, anyway, this Thomas Beecham? And how could I know who wrote the music? Or what it was called? Poor Doffie didn't know about ordinary children, I suppose. I felt about as big as a squashed ant and managed to stifle another sigh but couldn't stop hiccoughs, which irritated her even more and mortified me.

But before there was a chance to read anything, something magical happened. The whole place went dark and far below us, to roars of welcoming applause, a shaft of light picked up the small figure of a man and followed him into the circle of light on the podium. He bowed to us all. Then he lifted his baton and waited—quite a long time until there wasn't the slightest sound. Then everyone stood as he conducted "God Save the King." Once again after we were seated, he waited for silence before he would begin the concert.

The music rose up to us rich and clear, but nothing they played was at all familiar to me. Everyone else recognized them and clapped a lot after each piece. Beside me, I could hear Doffie singing along happily whenever she knew the melody. Sir Thomas put on a lively show which everybody obviously enjoyed. I came away full of new feelings and sounds and from then on paid special attention to overtures because they geared up my excitement for whatever was to happen in the ensuing show.

Not knowing anything at all at that first concert, not even the name of the conductor, I must have frustrated Doffie with my naivete, but she didn't give up. Time and again we saw productions at the Albert Hall, sometimes with stages built over parts of the seating, sometimes with animals taking part, sometimes massed choirs. Mostly I remember Handel's *Messiah* and *Hiawatha*. I got the feeling that in those days everyone in England loved theatre in some form and I still believe that was the case.

A favourite place to sit with a lunch package was at the "Old Vic," watching the development of my idol, Laurence Olivier. He had a special way of saying lines that was like no one else—clipped staccato, fast as a woodpecker—but his words, rippling and rolling from his tongue, were so distinct and clear that any child could understand their meaning. Listening to his silver voice among those many others who played uncut versions—as long as four hours—of *Hamlet*, *Henry V*, *Richard III*, *Romeo and Juliet* and *The Merchant of Venice*—I fell in love with him in that dark old theatre with its narrow, rickety seats on uncarpeted floor. Because we students attended in the afternoons, we got good seats right up close to the actors. We could hear them breathe and see them sweat while, physically as well as emotionally, they propelled themselves through those demanding roles. The elaborate stage action that required duelling, falling down stairs and climbing battlements never ceased to amaze me. And no one did it like Olivier. He was bound for fame.

At the same time, Noel Coward's musicals were making headlines, one after another, and the American Blackbird Company paid London annual visits with a new blockbuster for each season. (I especially enjoyed the skinny, black Nicholas Brothers.) We saw them all, including as many European and Middle Eastern companies as we could squeeze in evenings for. Occasionally we had good seats but more often, having queued outside—sometimes for hours on a two-and-sixpenny folding stool—Doffie and I would climb to "the gods"—much noisy huffing and puffing—for a sixpenny seat. *Good old Aunty!* I can't imagine how she could bear it, but she was as keen as I and terribly knowledgeable about every facet of theatre. I think my enthusiasm must have been her payment for many an aching back, poor darling. But even though I soon became aware that my cultural diet was richer than most children ever have the good fortune to experience, it took me a long time to fully appreciate the quality of the nourishment she put before me.

When the Old Victoria company joined with the Sadler's Wells opera and ballet company, the "Vic-Wells" was born, and by that time I had become one of the regulars in the gods. I roared and shouted with all the other students and housewives and old-agers to let the artists know how we felt: "Bravo!" or "Good try!" or "What happened?" They, in turn, performed for us, bowed to us, and usually received our enthusiastic support.

Although my free days in London were few, Doffie and I walked to the King's Road where she pointed out the Pheasantry, the artists' club to which she belonged. It was there, she said, that Alicia Markova and Anton Dolin had both studied as children under the tutelage of a Russian princess called Seraphine Astafieva. And at Glebe Place, only a few blocks from Cheyne Cottage, she showed me the enchanting property, like a little park tucked behind wrought iron railings, shrubs and delicate trees, where Anton Dolin's private dance studio was presently located. Sometimes we crossed the Thames River via Albert Bridge to enjoy Battersea Park.

And there was street entertainment as well. In Montreal on our way to England I had been hit hard by the sight of beggars on the street and had felt so sorry for a man sitting cap in hand on the pavement that I had wanted to give him all my worldly wealth—a few dollars—but Doffrey had stopped me. Here in London, a happy lot of panhandlers gave the crowd something to willingly pay them for. The Pearly Kings and Queens, despite their costumes being old and ragged sometimes, were a clever lot who entertained wherever there was a queue and, so I was told, "made pots of money." Sometimes, if it was a burlesque or vaudeville that we were waiting to see, the show outside was better than the one inside the theatre.

I can't imagine now how we did it all, but I dare say there wasn't a museum or art gallery, nor a church or theatre in London that Doffie and I missed. She took me to Madame Tussaud's Waxworks, the Knights Chapel and the Inner Temple. Some of it must have rubbed off on me, but I have to admit there came a time when I could not take in anything more. For years afterwards I wouldn't go near a museum. Other things also became tiresome to me: the smell of fog, traffic jams, coal dust and the hard, hard water.

# 7
# MALCOLM

*L*ondon headquarters of the Bank of Montreal at #9 Waterloo Place, SW1, was a post office for many Canadians who knew they could trust it to deal with "please forward" requests. When necessary, the bank even acted as next-of-kin. Thus it had become a haven for Doffie and, because of Grandfather Sweeny, everyone in the bank knew her. She expected service there, and she got it. I am also sure that she twisted the loan clerks around her little finger when she had overspent on me or on partying.

Who knows how much my ballet tuition cost her and how much she paid out for me to enter dance competitions? And then there were doctor and dentist bills. Because my natural teeth did nothing to enhance my appearance, Doffie took me to a dentist in Harley Street, the most expensive location for this sort of professional, to get them straightened. This doctor was a charlatan to be sure, because although he fitted my poor mouth with a whole plate over its roof and gold bands around the front teeth with great hooks that tore into my cheeks, in the two years that I wore the contraption without complaint or failure—dancing, performing or on holiday—he never put pressure on the hooks. And nothing changed at all.

My hands were another problem. Soon after my arrival we had been to a doctor about my warts. He tried caustic which blackened them but obviously didn't get to the root. An intern Doffie knew suggested the new carbon-dioxide-snow method; this produced huge blisters to remove the warts, but as the resulting sores healed, the warts began to grow again.

I was also prone to aches and nausea from the time I set foot in England, and one night sometime within the first few months, I had been wakened by an intense chest pain that felt like tight steel wires binding me. It lasted an hour or so but I didn't disturb anyone. In the morning I mentioned it to Doffrey who said it was probably indigestion. Perhaps so, but I haven't forgotten the fear. From time to time as the months passed, my complaints of tummy aches landed me in a specialist's office where the prodding was painful enough to assure me I had appendicitis. But no, I was just growing up, they said. Dance training would kill or cure me.

When times were good—that is, when Doffie had collected some dividends—she and I went on shopping sprees. Costume-fabric shops or ballet-shoe shops appealed to Doffie and me alike. She loved buying things for me like my make-up box and Leichner's grease paint, *pointe* shoes and character shoes, anything to do with my career. I sometimes wished we had more time to spend at Fortnum & Mason, Swan & Edgar, Harrods and Liberty, but they were horribly expensive.

Mostly Doffie and I shopped with amusement and enthusiasm, but there were days—after a party or when she had been coughing all night—when her patience was noticeably thin and I knew to expect trouble. On one occasion when a clerk in Swan & Edgar displeased her, Doffie, swearing a blue streak, rapped the glass-topped counter with her stick and threatened to have the poor woman expelled. As usual on those occasions, I tried to pretend she didn't belong to me, but she always called me to her side. "Where were you off to? We have business here. What was it you wanted? Why did you bring us here?" By this time I'd have forgotten the measurement of the elastic I needed or couldn't think what other items had been on our list.

During good times, Doffie and I both had weekly haircuts by a well-known hairdresser on Bond Street. When he had cut and washed and dried my mop, he used a flaming taper, the same as he had done for Doffie, to smooth off the prickly ends. This didn't mean that Monsieur Whoever-He-Was ever made me look like a dancer. My red frizz continued to be red frizz. And all this must have cost a penny, but it was more nonsense that I loved.

*Malcolm Campbell Sweeny*

The winter I was twelve, however, I was still wearing the green woollen dress and brown tweed coat bought in Vancouver and the brown leggings Doffie had bought. It wasn't till March 1935, when my arms had grown inches too long for the green dress, that Doffie finally bought me a new wardrobe. The country cousins in Scotland couldn't believe it when I turned up with a whole trunk full of clothes for the summer holiday. I was quite embarrassed, but at least I now had a choice when the housemaid asked what she should "lay out" for dinner, and I had more than one pair of shoes for John, the footman, to shine. I took to such service without shame.

My brother Malcolm, however, did not like that kind of nonsense at all. He had arrived in London in September 1934, after working his way on a tramp steamer via the Panama Canal from Vancouver. Malcolm was fifteen and had come to England to fulfil his dream of going to sea as a real sailor. He stayed with us at the cottage for a few days and we had fun going with Doffie to the City of London where, after buying his uniform and other gear he would need as a naval cadet, we toured the Tower. Then my dance term began and Malcolm joined HMS *Worcester*, an old sailing ship that lay in the Thames at Greenhithe where it was used as the merchant-marine training school. On a couple of Sundays, Doffie took me down there by bus for tea aboard ship, an event known among the cadets as a "bun fight." Guests were taken out to the ship by cutter.

At one of these *Worcester* bun fights I met a gorgeous young cadet whom Malcolm said was the ex-crown prince of Persia, Prince Hamid Kedjar. I told my friend Mary Sterling about him, and together we made plans to skip dance classes one Saturday afternoon to see Malcolm—and hopefully the prince. For several weeks we schemed and saved our shillings to have hair-dos and manicures (I chose black polish). On the appointed lunch break, the two of us took the series of busses necessary to reach Greenhithe, but on that jaunt Mary and I didn't even get aboard, having arrived too late for visitors. However, I imagined I caught sight of Hamid in the cutter going back to the ship. I never found out who told Doffie, but I lost my allowance for a month and Mary was properly grounded. Not particularly courageous, I didn't plan anything so daring again for a very long time.

On his first leave Malcolm returned to London where he and I made quite a flurry at a Grosvenor House young people's Christmas party. Someone had given us tickets, and whoever it was also delivered us by taxi. My brother seemed suddenly to have grown up. I'd forgotten, or never given it a thought, that he was awfully good-looking. His once blonde curly hair was going dark, though the lashes surrounding his quiet blue eyes had always been thick and black. His slow-to-start smile was as warm as a hug. And in the dress uniform of a merchant navy cadet he looked smashing. I was terribly proud of him and felt ever so grown up at twelve-and-a-half in my first full-length gown. It was emerald velvet, adorned only by a thick silver cord that, circling my waist, fell to the hem with two heavy tassels. My shiny red mop must have contrasted alarmingly with the green of my dress, but to my surprise I won the prize for prettiest hair!

Malcolm went with me at Easter 1935 to spend the holidays at Makerstoun, but he was appalled by its grandiosity, by the gross snobbery, by J.J. and Djan, by their way of speaking to people, by the fawning of footmen. I took him to the rabbit warrens and fishing holes, to the stables and kennels and to Cousin Eva's garden, hoping to win his approval, but he couldn't wait to get away from what he called "a sick atmosphere." I was disappointed in him, although at the same time I felt guilty for having fallen so easily under the spell of the Scottish relatives.

Shortly after that Makerstoun holiday, Doffie and Doffrey (who was still studying in London though by then no longer living with us) thought up a great plan for visiting Malcolm. They would rent a car one Sunday, we would take a lunch basket and be at the dock when the cadets came ashore for the afternoon.

Hooray! I thought.

But when Sunday came, Doffie was late getting up, and Doffrey, who was in charge of getting the car, was an hour late arriving because she had not finalized arrangements to collect it. Up at the crack of dawn myself, I had dressed and made the sandwiches, but even when Doffrey turned up, I couldn't hurry either of the women. At least two sickening hours went by before we set off, neither of them sure which road to take out of London.

They were in fine spirits, whooping it up every time they recognized a sign post on the road or saw some village pub whose brew they wished to sample. Left sitting crouched in the back of a very small car, I felt as though they had not only forgotten me but also the purpose of the journey. Once in a while they would seem intent on finding Greenhithe, with Doffie holding her glasses (minus one tine) to read the map, but then they'd get lost again. Noon came and went. I could picture Malcolm sitting alone on the dock, all the other cadets having been collected. He would not be angry, but I

*Refurbished and painted white, Makerstoun, 63 years after Malcolm's visit, remains a laird's manor, perched above the Tweed.*

was, and there was nothing I could do. My frustration grew as these two women laughed their way through the afternoon. We finally arrived at dockside around five o'clock, just in time to see my brother climb aboard the cutter that took the last lads back to the ship.

With my heart breaking for poor Malcolm, I rode all the way back to Chelsea in a cold rage. Treating me as though I didn't exist hurt enough, but I couldn't believe the callous behaviour that my aunt and her friend had shown toward my brother. Though I always admired her, I didn't always love my Aunt Dorothea.

The excitement of having Malcolm and the *Worcester* in my life on top of the rigours of my dance studies was probably too much for one so young. I was growing fast and I felt tired more and more often. My stomach aches persisted and sometimes I got terrible colds. I wasn't looking well. Even Malcolm mentioned it in a letter to Mum. But my elementary exam was coming up soon. I had no time to indulge myself in illness.

In the meantime, that spring Malcolm had received a letter from Dad in which he relayed an invitation from an old army friend, Major N.M. Vibart, a Royal Engineers Yacht Club member who raced and cruised a vessel called *Altair*, berthed in Southampton. Vibart wanted a couple of lads, sixteen years of age, to complete the crew of this fourteen-ton sailing cutter for a family cruise to the Azores that summer. Could Malcolm take a longer than usual summer leave from *Worcester* for such a valuable experience? Permission was soon granted, but Malcolm was then torn between this opportunity for ocean sailing and the chance to "man the yards" with the other *Worcester* cadets on a training ship at the 1935 Spithead review. He chose the *Altair*.

While I sweated for my first major dance exam, my brother finished his year on *Worcester* and swatted up on deep-sea sailing. In late May, Doffie and I went shopping again with Malcolm who had a list of his needs for the tropics. I don't recall seeing him off when the *Altair* set sail in mid-June, being busy with exam preparations at the time. The whole voyage was to take approximately six weeks, so we didn't expect any word from him before mid-July when the ship should be well on her way home from the Azores.

While all these adventures were happening, my education had been continuing somewhat erratically. Miss Richardson had left at the end of July 1934 and been replaced in October by a younger woman who did try arithmetic and spelling. Unfortunately, she must have displeased Aunty because she stayed only a few months.

During the spring of 1935 I had been delivered every morning to the residence of two effeminate young men who lived in a most elaborately decorated house. It was dark panelled and hung with plum velvet draperies pulled back by tasselled gold cords. I sat at a huge, black dining room table to be tutored by first one, then the other, but I felt that teaching me was just a lark to them. I remember sensing their smirking presence behind me as I worked at the table. Aunty continued to take me to their house until, at the end of summer term in 1935, I said goodbye to education forever. I would be thirteen before the autumn term started again and, being a girl of that age, I would be allowed by the London County Council to dance all day.

The Royal Academy of Dancing elementary exam may sound easy, but the syllabus, though simple, was extremely demanding. Two examiners would be looking for good manners, a positive attitude and a good body. We were expected to display musicality in our presentation as well as physical strength and accuracy. We were to know the French vocabulary and to understand and answer detailed questions applicable to *barre* and centre work. By this stage of our training, we students should have achieved smooth and accurate carriage of arms and the proper use of hands, head and eyes. We had to perform a variety of single *pirouettes*, show speed and precision in picking up new *enchaînements* and hold an *arabesque* without wobbling. To complete the test, each of us would perform the short compulsory examination piece that we had rehearsed in advance.

At exam time, six of us at a time in alphabetical order would enter the large studio at Holland Park Avenue, dressed in short classical tutus with white socks and pink ballet slippers correctly tied. Our hair had to be either short or tied back firmly. For the smattering of boys, black tights, black shoes and a white shirt were obligatory.

Having passed the five children's grade exams in less than the two years prescribed, I was surprisingly nervous when, dressed and warmed up, with Doffie hovering, I waited my turn to take the elementary, my first major examination. Soon the group before mine would be coming out of the exam room. The music that accompanied the final solo test piece had begun for the fourth student, so I knew there were exactly four-and-a-half minutes left. For the fourth time I repeated the little dance in my head. Then did it a fifth time, then a sixth. After a few moments of quiet in the studio, the door opened and the six girls, rosy-cheeked and shiny, hurried back into the dressing room to explode into chatter as soon as the door was closed behind them. Another minute and the door opened again. The secretary called the next six names. Mine, beginning with *S*, left me as usual at the end of the line.

Entering widely spaced as we had been advised, each girl paused to curtsey in front of the examiners' table before taking her place at the *barre*. The examiners, Kathleen Daintree and Madame Adeline Genée, smiled at each of us in turn. Beginning to feel confident as I curtsied, I walked with head high to my place at the *barre*.

Although my turn-out and extensions were far from spectacular, I knew the *barre* work well and enjoyed it. When we moved to centre floor, I was first to put my hand up when we were asked to describe the eight points on a dancer's compass. I not only explained them but took the eight positions, four of them diagonals and four facing directly front, side, or back to the audience. This was more than they wanted because in the next exercise we went through the positions again. I felt stupid. I then managed to turn third position of arms in the wrong direction—of all the ridiculous errors! I could feel my face burn. Fortunately mine wasn't the only fault, and after a bit I settled down to work. The things I did best were with the upper part of my body, so I flowed fairly well through centre practice until *pirouettes*. There I lost my self-assurance again and fluffed landings several times. When we got to little steps and *batterie*, I thought I did really well and danced my heart out in the simple piece at the end.

The results were only so-so. The remark on my test report said my knees were too straight in *batterie*. I passed with eighty-two percent. No honours.

With Malcolm at sea and my elementary exam safely over, I was free to go again to visit Shum at Bankside. After only a couple of days of restful inactivity, she suggested we drive northeast to Lauderdale in Roxburghshire to attend a fete at Thirlestane Castle.

It is recorded that as far back as 1345 a castle called Thirlestane, seven miles from the village of Lauder, was the seat of the dukes of Maitland. The present castle, a massive red sandstone edifice close to the village, was begun in 1590, commissioned by the then current duke who wanted to have a greater say in the affairs of Lauder. The six-storey main block, reputed to have been built over an underground river, took six years to build. Two three-storey projecting bedroom wings were added later with three semi-circular stair towers on each wing—six in all—leading to the bedrooms.

I had been to Thirlestane a year earlier with the Ormrods on a trip I would not forget. The present inhabitant, Ian Colin Maitland, seventeenth Earl of Lauderdale, had married Marda Ormrod's sister, Ivy, who thus became the Countess of Lauderdale. Ian and Ivy, with their children, Lady Sylvia and Viscount Ivor, plus their maids and butler, lived in just a couple of dozen of the castle's ground-floor rooms. The remainder was closed off, presumably for economic reasons.

Olly and Teen had given me the grand tour, however, and I had found it exciting and creepy to explore the heights and depths of a sixteenth-century castle. We clumped up the curving stone stairways to each of the six towers. At the top of the sixth was a room that Olly said was a torture chamber. There were huge hooks around the walls, and a trap door in its floor that allowed prisoners to be dropped into the underground river. Or so Olly said.

Having climbed to the ramparts, we then descended stone steps beneath the kitchen on our way to investigate the nether regions. A single hanging electric bulb at the bottom of the stairway was all that lighted the steps and the narrow, earthen passageway where we must stoop to walk. This corridor had wooden doors on either side that creaked as we peered into the darkness of wine cellars and food storage rooms along the way. No doubt there were light switches inside the doors, but we didn't find them. After a hundred feet or so, the passage branched, and around the corner to the right a second hanging bulb illuminated the heavy, iron-barred gates of what appeared to be a dungeon. By then I'd had enough. I had no desire to enter a dungeon or to find the river. Olly laughed and said I was a poor sport.

Ian had invited the local gentry for a showing that afternoon of an amateur film he had taken on a visit to British Columbia during a recent round-the-world tour with his family. Because of the size of the expected audience, dank dust-sheets had been removed from some of the priceless antique furniture in an enormous, musty, main-floor reception room. The shuttered windows remained closed for the viewing, and it was so dark that, even with the door to the hallway open and minimal electric light, visitors could barely find the chairs and sofas.

Tallish, lean and loose-limbed, Ian wore his sandy-to-mousey receding hair slicked back from his high, pallid forehead. From below yellowish brows, his scrunched grey-blue eyes peered inquisitively. His hands were long and pale. He looked and smelled unwashed. He was the tweedy type, and from time to time I saw him in plus fours with knee socks and brogues, but he also owned much official clothing for

*Even in the 1930s the family only used the bottom floor of the castle.*

*Ivy, the Countess of Lauderdale bequeathed the castle to
her grandson, Captain Gerald Maitland-Carew (above) in 1972
and he gave the main part and contents of Thirlestane to the Trust
in 1984. Today Thirlestane (below) stands remote, at the centre
of a massive estate, now managed by a Charitable Trust and
maintained by the National Heritage Memorial Fund.*

military and governmental occasions which he kept in a
wardrobe near the back pantry. All of it was old and smelled
of stale sweat and moth balls. This was not an uncommon
smell for country people who lived among animals, inside
and out, in old, cold buildings that were unheated except for
the occasional tightly-sealed room where an open fireplace
burned wood and sometimes a lump of coal. There it was
possible to to get really hot and sweaty.

On the occasion of the film showing, Ian seemed determined that I should have the best seat, right next to his, since
the film included pictures of my own family at Pasley
Island. Once the crowd settled and the door was closed, he
suggested I might see even better if I sat upon his knee. Not
thrilled with the idea—I was twelve years old at that time—
but not wanting to offend his lordship, I did as bid and
watched in the flickering darkness as his photographic journey began to unfold.

I don't remember seeing Pasley in the film, however, or
any of my family because before long my concentration
focused on Ian's more-than-friendly hands which were
taking liberties I wasn't prepared for. Though he resisted, I
managed to get off his knee into the chair beside him. I was
glad of the darkness. No one could witness my horrible
embarrassment. As soon as the film was over, I fled from the
scene.

This memory was still vivid when dear Shum suggested
we attend the fete at Thirlestane Castle that summer in 1935.
How could I tell her I didn't want to go? So, packed for a
night away, off we drove.

The fete was like a whole village fair spread out on the
closely cropped lawns around the base of the benign-look-
ing, weathered-pink castle. Between flowerbeds on the lower
terraces, snow-white tents decked with little flags and
colourfully painted stalls filled with local produce gleamed
in bright sunshine. Barrows and horse-drawn waggons
displayed wares and crafts for sale. Shum gave me a couple
of pounds and sent me off to investigate. Chicks, ducks, sheep
and rabbits, even a litter of pink piglets amused me, but
despite the lovely day—a rarity in Scotland—and endless
inviting displays to interest me, my uneasiness about Ian
Maitland's proximity kept me cautious and alert. Once I came

face to face with him, said, "How d'you do," then turned rudely on my heel and walked away. After that I managed to keep out of his sight until Shum found me and we drove south to Makerstoun where we were to spend the night.

That evening I asked permission from Shum to telephone Aunty for news of Malcolm and *Altair*. "Sorry, my sweet," Doffie said, "there's no news yet."

Next day our hosts Djan and J.J., in two Rolls-Royces packed full of house guests and basket luncheons, set off for the Jedburgh Horse Show. J.J. paid a huge amount for ringside parking and we drove into slots right beside the Maitlands, who had come to join our picnic. I tried to be polite when Ian greeted me warmly, but as soon as possible ran away with Olly and Teen to find their friends at the stables.

"Lunch will be ready soon," called Djan. "Don't go far!"

When we returned, a sumptuous picnic was spread out on linen cloths on the grass, with more gourmet stuff available from baskets in the boots of the cars. The two chauffeurs doubled as footmen. Thinking to avoid Ian, I cut myself a wedge of Melton Mowbray pork pie and slipped inside a Rolls. Not a minute later he joined me. To avoid him, I made my exit by an opposite door with his lordship slithering after me. Thank goodness I could run. Quickly losing myself in the crowd, I watched the luncheon from a distance, tummy rumbling. It all looked so delicious. Why, I wondered, had Ian come to spoil my day again? Why was I so helpless? Why couldn't I bring myself to tell Shum what he had done?

I waited until it appeared that Djan was ready to leave. This didn't take long—she only "put in an appearance" at most events—and I arrived breathless just as she was sending someone to find me. Nothing was said about my absence. Several years later when I told Olly about my various adventures with Cousin Ian, he said, "Oh him! He's a dirty old man. Got put in the clink for chasing small boys. He's a fart!"

Next day Shum and I drove back to Bankside, and Doffie phoned to tell me she had the happy letter we had been awaiting from my brother. He had arrived in the Azores. It had taken almost three weeks longer than we had expected, but that was nothing to worry about in a sailing boat. Obviously recalling *The Tale of Two Cities* from his last term at St. George's,

Malcolm had written poetically about the ship, Captain Vibart and sailing the ocean. "It is a far, far better way of living," he penned, "than I could ever have dreamed."

After I returned to London in late August, I began expecting every day to hear that they were safely home. When friends asked, "What news of your brother?" I'd say, "Nothing yet. They may have been blown off course or something, but they're all fine sailors. They'll find their way!" or "They'll be along any day now."

But I was worried. Why weren't they back? September came and went without news. I wrote to Mum not to worry. Perhaps they were off course from a storm. Then we heard about a tidal wave and the failure, for the first time in a hundred years, of the trade winds. Of course, we said, they must have been becalmed. Nobody actually suggested to me that the ship could have been sunk.

*Altair* still hadn't returned when in early October I went again to stay with Shum. This time she rented a pony for me from the local riding stable. I thought it was the loveliest thing I had ever seen. "It's dead," she said. "They fed it on sawdust!"

Dead? Not by a long shot. My poor behind! That pony was a terrible handful. Had I really known how to ride I could have had a great time, but he scared me in the hunting field because he always wanted to be out in front—even in front of the whippers-in! These individuals, also known as whips, are the experienced members of the hunt club who assist the master and the huntsman in training the hounds. Their title comes from the whips which they use to concentrate the hounds in a tight pack or bring back strays. They ride between the pack and the field—that is, the riders involved in the chase—to make sure no overly eager rider crosses the scent of the fox.

Shum's groom, Henry, had probably been told to look after me. He took a lot of time showing me how to clean the stable, the pony's feet and his tack, and he showed me how to lead a pony about properly. Henry and I became great friends, and over the years he sowed in me the seeds of horsemanship. In fact, it was the stable management and basic riding skills he taught me that gave me the confidence years later to organize and become district commissioner for the

Langley branch of the Canadian Pony Club. But that's another story.

Returning to London again, I studied and rehearsed late for competitions. As autumn dragged on into winter, everyone was kind to me, giving me things to do to keep me from thinking of Malcolm. They no longer asked, "What news?" I wrote and wrote to Dad and Mum but hardly mentioned the thing I dared not seriously contemplate.

By keeping my nose to the grindstone, I was ready to enter several balletic classes in the All-England Sunshine Dancing Competition, sponsored by the Sunshine Homes for Blind Babies. This was a nation-wide, biannual event consisting of municipal heats, provincial semi-finals and then finals in London. Phyllis Bedells' School of Dancing always did well in solo, *pas de deux*, and group categories in these competitions.

But by now I seemed to have a permanent cold. For a rest, Aunty sent me to Rycott for a weekend with old Mrs. Hamersley, whose children had been my mother's school friends. I had visited her during spring the previous year. Now at Rycott the beech leaves had fallen, covering the floor of the wood I had last seen carpeted in bluebells. No shred was left of the wild daffodils I remembered picking within the grounds of an ancient stone chapel. Due to the age and immensity of trees surrounding it, even Rycott itself seemed darker than when I had first visited, and my room was lightless and chilly.

Because Doffie knew that I suffered not knowing Malcolm's fate, she kept my days full, sending me here and there whenever any short break came. But these trips did nothing to allay my fears or relieve a permanent pain—about which I never spoke—that sat just below the surface of my consciousness. *Do they still believe there is hope?* I asked myself, although I never dared ask it aloud.

With Christmas approaching, I was additionally saddened by news of the king's serious illness, and on January 21, 1936, all schools closed when it was announced that King George V had died. On January 24, Doffie asked me if I would accompany her next day to pay our respects to the late king whose body had been brought to London from Sandringham to lie in state at Westminster Hall.

"How long will it take?" I asked.

"O-o-o-oh, several hours, I expect. I think it would be a valuable experience for you."

I was ready when she came downstairs surprisingly early next morning. Doffie put knitted socks over her lisle stockings and dug out her oldest, most comfortable oxfords while I boiled us an egg and made toast. As the day was mild for the time of year although heavily overcast, we went on foot along the embankment to catch a taxi, but we had driven only a short distance after crossing Vauxhall Bridge to the south side of the Thames before we came upon the perhaps twenty-abreast queue inching its way along the Albert Embankment toward Westminster Bridge. The sight of so many human beings shuffling patiently in one direction with a single thought in mind, to catch a close-up glimpse of the face of the dead monarch, had a powerful effect on me. We left the taxi and became official mourners. The many times I had been in a church, with my parents or alone, became one with the new feeling of respect and reverence this occasion evoked. I felt other-worldly in a place that was lonely and sad. And for once, Doffie seemed to be there, too. I wondered if hers was as much an act of grieving for Malcolm as it was for the king. I know mine was.

As the day wore on, I remember how weary I became, but for her, with nowhere to lean or rest, the journey must have been particularly uncomfortable. She showed her real strength by staying cheery and good-natured the entire route. It took fully six hours of moving at a snail's pace—no one pushed, no queue buskers entertained—to reach and cross Westminster Bridge and arrive at the doors of Westminster Hall. Once there, no one could wish to hurry. Reduced to four abreast as we entered, we divided again to walk two each side of the catafalque. Feeling quite separate and alone, I took my feelings to the old man's bier and left them there for him. *Please take care of my brother.*

Next day Doffie put me on a train to Bedford to stay with my friend Phyllis Dakin. Without asking anyone's advice or permission, the two of us decided to go up to London on January 29 to watch the solemn funeral procession pass on its way to Paddington Station en route to the king's burial in Windsor Chapel. Hours ahead of the published time, we set off with biscuits and apples in our pockets. From the Oxford Street underground station, we crossed the Marble Arch intersection and found a space inside the iron railings of Hyde Park closest to the arch through which the procession was to pass. From our safe distance we watched as police took positions facing outward on either side of the arch. Beyond our railings, masses of people moved in between us and the police, thus diminishing our hope of a clear view, although a space of roped-off empty pavement remained immediately in front of us. In any case, we figured we could climb on the cement base of the railings and, holding onto them, be able to see everything.

The crowd grew more and more dense. Those who stood behind us were soon breathing down our necks. When St. John's ambulance personnel brought a stretcher bearing a passed-out woman, then a man with a greenish look, and laid them on the bare pavement in front of us, we discovered why the area had been roped off. Meanwhile, a whole company of soldiers had been marching into place behind the backs of the police and were taking up positions facing the arch.

It wasn't still enough to hear the birds, but with no traffic moving, a low thrum of human voices was carried on the light breeze which here and there lifted a scarf or flipped a collar. Then from the direction of Hyde Park Corner came the first low roar of voices and we all strained our ears and eyes. Sharp military orders brought the Marble Arch guard to attention. We couldn't see them, but we heard the thud of boots and the metallic clank of rifles hitting shoulders. By now distant drums could be heard and the muted voices of thousands of people.

"They're coming. Can you hear? They're coming!"

A young man pushed through from behind us and climbed up the railings. Several angry people tried to pull him down, but he hung on so strongly that they tore clothes off him before they dragged him down among them. Phyllis and I became separated in the scuffle. There was no way for us to get back together, though she answered the first time I called to her. The drums came closer. A pipe band played a musical lament. I heard marching feet, then the clop, clop of many horses and jangling of harness. The procession began to pass through the arch, and for probably thirty minutes after that, feet marched, horses drew carriages, marching bands played funeral dirges and more drummers beat out the same measured pace. I thought I caught sight of the tips of the golden spikes on the Horse Guard's helmets as they disappeared within the arch and re-emerged from it. I was sure they would be just ahead of the gun-carriage borne through the streets, as we had been told it would be, by one hundred men of the Royal Navy.

As the last drum beats faded far up Edgware Road, the soldiers and police near us were ordered to re-position for handling the crowd. We all turned our heads in the direction from which we had come, but none of us could move our bodies at all. Suddenly a pressure moved me and everyone around me sideways, en masse, along the railings toward an open gate that led out of Hyde Park into the centre of Marble Arch. Body tight to body, we were forced to run. Pushed from beside and behind, we were swirled toward the gateposts. I hit the policeman who had placed himself against that post to take the brunt of us, and we spun past him and out like lava that slowed only when more people came from the other direction.

There must have been many thousands at Marble Arch that day, and all of us seemed determined to cross the intersection in every direction at the same time, which meant that no one could move, or we all moved, sometimes slowly, sometimes in a rush, keeping our feet moving whichever way we were pushed. At one time when the rushing stopped, I stood petrified, squashed between upright bodies for about ten minutes. In the mob around me, several people had passed out, but they couldn't fall down.

Eventually enough people were pushed into the streets leading away from the intersection that the pressure relaxed in the centre, and people could hold up those who had fainted or at least lay them on the ground. At last I became part of the crowd that arrived at the Oxford Street underground to wait for trains.

It was pitch dark when by a stroke of luck Phyllis and I arrived back at Bedford station on the same train. Everyone at the Dakins' house had been listening to the wireless and had learned how thousands of the king's grieving subjects had flocked into London from the counties to say farewell to their sovereign. This had caused catastrophic roadblocks and hundreds of people had been trampled, some to death. Mrs. Dakin led the telling-off that we received, but it fell on dull ears. I already knew we had been stupid. I knew we were lucky to be safely home, but how could we have imagined such an event in advance? I never told my aunt what Phyllis and I had done.

*Verity dances in her parents' garden in North Vancouver on her visit home in 1936.*

# 8
## HOME FOR THE SUMMER

*D*uring the spring of 1936 I was very tired. My mouth was sore from the ill-fitting orthodontic plate and the hooks on the wires on my teeth. I had tummy aches and growing pains and one cold after another. The doctor said I should have my tonsils out, and after Doffie wrote to Mum with this news, plans were made for me to spend the summer of 1936 in Vancouver to have the operation done there. In the meantime Cousin Marda invited me to Wales during Olly's school holidays. I knew it was yet another diversion.

It seems to me that all that my cousins thought about in those days was hunting—fox hunting, otter hunting or deer hunting. For each quarry they sought, the field followed a particular pack of hounds bred especially for hunting the kind of territory in which those animals made their home. The field that followed foxhounds over farm land rode horses. Those who followed otter hounds did their best to keep up on foot along the rivers. Deer hunters, also on foot, followed deerhounds in hilly country and through forests.

Fox hunting, the most prestigious and popular sport, was at least partly so because of the swank of hunting attire and partly because of the snobby social gatherings where riders could admire each other on immaculately turned-out mounts. Full dress for the executive members of a mounted hunt included black boots cuffed under the knee with four inches of light brown leather, snow-white britches (often of glove leather), white gloves, black velvet hunt caps or silk toppers and gold-buttoned, scarlet coats with black velvet collars. These red coats, known as "Pinks" after the master tailor who had designed the original, were worn over white shirts with folded stiff white stocks under the chin.

When correctly dressed for a hunt, the field would turn out in fawn or white britches with black boots and jackets, white stocks, white gloves and black hats. Minute yellow or red waistcoats were rare, but permissible. Generally, each local hunt club was supported by the gentlemen farmers and important landowners of the county. Dues-paying members received a programme of the season's hunts and were invited to bring along a friend when they attended a ten o'clock "meet with the hounds," usually in a courtyard or in front of a grand manor or castle on one of the estates. Here everyone chatted and showed off as they downed a tot of strong booze prior to actually hunting their host's foxes. The hounds moved off precisely at eleven o'clock. To close the season, someone would host a grand Hunt Ball.

Each spring, however, before the season's opening hunt, a scruffy but dedicated collection of riders would set out, literally before the crack of dawn, on a mission they called "cubbing" which was a training time for green horses, young and inexperienced riders and the newest generation of hounds. It was a time for learning good manners in the hunting field. It was also an opportunity for elderly riders to enjoy being out with their friends without having to face the challenge of a full chase.

Visiting Coed-y-Glynn that spring, I was lent old brown breeks, a tweed jacket, brown boots that were too big for me, and a shabby black hunting cap in preparation for cubbing the following day. At five in the morning dear Da hauled us out of our beds. I put on my borrowed finery and joined Olly and Teen, dressed in their tweeds, for breakfast. We ate almost in silence and got out to the cobbled stableyard while it was still dark.

The family groom, Eric Alderson, was already bringing from the stable a big bay gelding, tacked up, ready to mount. This was the horse Marda had rented for me from what she called "the local horse trader." As neatly as I could, I swung into the grown-up saddle. It was a long way to the ground from the huge, unfamiliar creature on which I now sat.

Trying to appear nonchalant, I checked my stirrups. Then looking up, I saw an apparition walking across the stable yard. It was Marda wearing an ancient black riding habit. In one hand she carried a crop and with the other she dragged the trailing end of her sidesaddle skirt. On her head was a shiny black topper. A black veil, covering her hat and face, was tied beneath her chin.

Like Shum, Marda had been born in the era before women rode astride. Although she could not have been over forty, she seemed older than that, and I had assumed she no longer rode. She must have decided to come along at the last minute, and this was probably the only riding outfit she owned. Alderson had already put the tack on Tara, an old mare that I had understood was long ago retired, and he was bringing her forward when I thought I saw her lurch under the weight of a monstrous sidesaddle.

Tipping his cap to his mistress, Alderson held Tara close to a mounting block while Marda walked up the steps. Gripping the curved knee-hooks on the saddle, she backed onto it. The mare shuddered. If Marda noticed, she gave no sign, but hooking her right knee over the pommel, she pulled the full part of the skirt up over her knee before buttoning it to her waist. Obediently, as soon as she felt the reins gathered up, Tara walked away from the mounting block.

While Olly finished tacking up his new mount, Lucy Grey in the stable, Alderson brought out his own horse, along with the pony Tootles, all ready for Teen who popped up lightly.

"Master Oliver will be with us at any moment, Madam," Alderson announced as he checked Teen's stirrups and sprang into his own saddle. "We may as well move off now." Tootles whinnied to Lucy Grey, who returned the greeting from the stable as Alderson, with Teen's pony on a lead rope beside him, led the way out of the stableyard, followed by Marda, then me. Olly soon trotted up, and Tootles twisted around squealing as Lucy Grey approached her from behind and passed by to ride in front of all of us. At that time in the morning no one had much to say, but the sleepy clop-clip-clop of twenty horseshoes on a country road was chatter enough to calm my ever-anxious insides.

As the sky became light, we left the road through a gate in a hedge and followed other riders down a track between an evergreen wood and a ploughed field. It was now six a.m. Perhaps forty riders, some of them having already "hacked" five or more miles, had assembled at the site of the meet, a picturesque clearing in the woods where a mist had begun to rise.

The well-warmed horses and ponies were ready for a bit of a gallop, but no, this was neither the time nor the place for it. "Ho!" "Settle down!" "Behave, damn you!" could be heard as obstreperous mounts, excited by the presence of strange horses, were brought into line. Red ribbons braided into some of the horses' tails warned that they kicked. I made sure to keep my distance.

The animals had barely settled down when the huntsman arrived on the other side of the clearing with a huge pack of lively hounds and the fidgeting began all over again. Most of the hounds were young and inquisitive, and some of the youngest had been coupled to old hounds that would teach them the rules. The huntsman and several whippers-in took their places surrounding the pack, using their whips to keep them together. Although they used low voices, they snapped sharp commands at the hounds if they disobeyed.

On our side of the clearing the field of riders grouped close together to receive the same sort of discipline from the hunt master. "Respect the farmers' fields. Don't crowd the fences. Never get in front of the hounds. Don't yell unless you actually see a fox. Be patient with your mounts at this time of year and don't raise your voices. Teach them to stand quietly while waiting for cubs to come out of the den to play. If a cub runs off, the hounds, given the signal, must learn to follow the scent." The idea was not to kill the cubs but to scatter them and to pick up only one scent. This meant that the field might have to wait some time for any action.

With his instructions complete, the master left the riders talking quietly to each other and to their mounts, and he, the huntsman and whippers-in moved the hound pack through the wood and out of sight.

The children and horses soon became impatient, and Olly deliberately took his mount away from her stable mate, Tootles, knowing that Lucy Grey would whinny and put on her act of rearing and bucking like a rocking horse, while Teen—completely fearless although only seven—laughed as

Tootles screamed and pawed the ground even though she was firmly held by Alderson mounted on his huge, well-behaved bay. I was embarrassed by their behaviour, but the Ormrods, being who they were, got away with it.

Hardly had Olly been chastised and things settled down, when I heard a great whacking of crop on flank and Marda's angry voice. "Tara! Wake up, you fool! Don't give me that old-age nonsense. Get up! Bitch!" Her horse had closed its eyes and was about to lie down under the weight of the sidesaddle.

At that moment a whip galloped out of the wood toward us. As he swung around to his left, he indicated with his crop that we should follow him to where the hounds were onto a scent. We hurried our horses after him, jostling for a safe position in the open and for a glimpse of the fast-moving hounds. Turning to watch Marda urging the reluctant Tara on, I nearly lost a stirrup and came down hard on my saddle a couple of times. As the last of us headed downhill around the copse, I caught sight of Marda scrambling off Tara as the old mare simply sat down.

The field had a short run across stubble to where a shallow stream ran around the base of a little hill. The mixed bag of horses and ponies took the stream in stride and followed a path over the crest, disappearing from sight. My mount, however, was having nothing of it. I kicked and smacked but he wouldn't go forward. We turned away and made another approach without success. After a minute or two a rescuer took my reins and tried to lead the beast—whose mother must have told him not to get his feet wet—through the stream. Finally, on my rescuer's advice, I slid off and held both horses (an unnerving moment) while my friend mounted and took command of mine. Still attached to me, the rotten animal jumped a mile in the air, sending me flying across the water. I thought I would be trampled by the other horse, but all was well. At least we were now on the other side where the chap held my horse for me to remount. I felt like an awful fool. Never mind. We hadn't far to go before running into the rest of the riders, who were becalmed again. Then a short run took us to the edge of another wood. The go-stop performance was repeated time and again until we finally returned to the place of the meet to find Marda sitting

153

half-asleep under a tree, holding Tara's reins. She must have been pleased to see Alderson, but angry because he hadn't been there when she needed him.

The summer term in England lasts until the end of July, but although I had started *pointe* work in May in preparation for my intermediate exam, I hadn't much enthusiasm for study. I knew I would be leaving for Vancouver at the end of the month because that was when Doffrey Findlay planned to return to Canada. Tickets had been bought for the two of us on the *Berengaria*. This time we would travel steerage because once again Doffie was short of funds. Our inside cabin was on E deck. Our dining hall was over the engines.

When the time came, I wasn't at all sure I wanted to go home. Even though no one had ever admitted that he could be dead, I kept feeling waves of anger about the way life had treated Malcolm. I knew Mum would be very sad. I must have thought Dad was able to take care of his own feelings,

*Berengaria 1921*

not knowing then how hard Malcolm's loss had hit him. He was a very private man who held his own pain close to himself. He never told his children how lonely he had been when he was sent away to boarding school as a little boy. He never spoke of the horrors of losing almost his whole company of engineers in a single battle in France during World War I, or about having been twice wounded. He never complained about doing poorly paid jobs far from home in order to feed us. At times he seemed distant, but he was always thinking about his family, as I learned from a letter he had written to me from Anyox on July 2, 1923. I was only a year old at the time, but Mum saved it for me and gave it to me after his death in 1940. It read in part:

> *What will you be able to think of your Dad when you grow up to understand? What will I be able to tell you of the glories of life? How am I going to make everything beautiful for you so that your sweetness can make your whole being beautiful? That I want you to be beautifully good is the bed- rock of it all, to grow up a really beautiful being. It is the incentive that I must stimulate in myself that matters. It is the control of myself and striving so that the beauty of your mother is available for your upbringing and that it is not lost in enervating anxiety to keep things going because I'm not big enough to take the burden all myself.*

Despite my uncertainty about going home, Doffrey was as cheerful as ever. Having done very well with her studies, she had a great future ahead of her. Now it was time for a holiday. I wasn't aware till after we had boarded that Doffrey was having something of an affair with Louy Regal, a well-known French muralist and friend of Doffie's, and that he would also be travelling with us. Louy, younger than Doffrey, appeared much the same as other artists I had met in Chelsea—serious, introverted and lonely. Though I saw little of him, I quite liked him. He and Doffrey seemed enchanted with each other, going about on deck arm-in-arm, oblivious of me.

Tired and still grieving, I preferred solitude. The trip wasn't too rough—I wasn't actually sick—although it was sometimes difficult not to be affected by the behaviour of the hundreds of immigrant passengers I observed who ate enormously and drank gallons of red wine, then threw it all up in the scuppers after every meal before another round of boisterous singing.

Everyone pointed out the Statue of Liberty as we sailed into New York harbour, and everyone oo-oo-ed and ah-ed at the skyline. We spent a couple of days in the big city. Except for forays out of the hotel to eat and drink all the things like sodas and juice and nuts that hadn't been available in London, I remained in our shoddy room to get some sleep while Doffrey and Louy did the sights. Then we boarded a bus and set out for Chicago, with me continuing to gorge on fruits and veggies at every stop, not realizing what I was doing to my stomach. Two days out from Chicago, as we crossed a barren stretch on the way to Salt Lake City, I got cramps and badly needed a bathroom. Unfortunately for me, bathrooms were not a feature of busses in those days. I won't describe the embarrassing situation further, but I can assure you I stopped eating altogether for several days and laid low while the other two took stock of each of the cities where we stayed for a day or two along the way. We had reached Salt Lake City before I felt better, and then I wanted to hurry home because we were already running later than had been predicted. I knew Mum would be worrying, but Salt Lake City was too important a sight for Doffrey and Louy to hurry through. "Stop worrying," Doffrey told me. No one expected anyone to arrive exactly on time from such a journey. And so I fretted and stayed in the hotel, feeling lonely and invisible.

About four days later we arrived in Vancouver, where my eldest brother picked me up from the bus station in Dad's old Green Misery. Sedley was home from military college in Ontario, thanks to the generous gift of his train-fare from the head of St. George's school. He dropped me off at the house in North Vancouver where Mum waited.

Approaching a little gate that stood open, I watched her walk toward me from the foot of the wooden steps down a path that crossed the lawn in front of the house. She looked so small. Her once dark hair was silver now. Just inside the gate we met.

"Look!" Mum said, reaching for the branch of a small lilac bush so heavy with flowers it had broken and was hanging sadly. "It was so beautiful, so young and strong, but it couldn't wait," she sobbed. "It just couldn't wait any longer."

We held each other and cried, and I knew that not all of our tears were for the joy of my homecoming.

Where was Dad? Teaching. Where was five-year-old Roger? Already in bed. Where was Moira? At some school function. Why hadn't Sedley come in with me? Perhaps he had to take the car back. I missed them. I needed them.

The house I had come home to in North Vancouver was old and friendly. Much of the facade was covered with roses and wisteria, but it looked as though neither had been pruned for some time. Beside the house, grass lay green between fruit trees, and from the veranda there was an unobstructed view of Vancouver's harbour. The place belonged to Coggie Buttar; she and her husband had been great gardeners, but after Coggie had been widowed, she had gone to live with her sister Kathleen, my Uncle Dick's wife. I suspect the rent Dad paid was minimal. It had to be.

Although I had only spent a few nights at the North Vancouver house before my trip to England, I remembered that the attic bedroom where I slept with my young sister Moira had been unfinished. Now she and Mum had painted it prettily in honour of my return, pale blue with white clouds on the ceiling. The two beds had pink spreads and there were two pale blue chests of drawers. The room was large and it had a good wooden floor, making a reasonably spacious studio for my dance practice.

Moira lived her life in my shadow and had been taking dance lessons to better understand my studies. Although she was not a very capable performer, I found her extremely knowledgeable about the history of dance and who was currently who in the dance world. She was far ahead of me in music generally and had collected records and ballet scores. That summer we not only practised ballet but also jazz and tap.

One day, when I was happily stepping out a soft-shoe routine to a popular record, my mother called upstairs in a pain-filled voice. "Verity, Verity! How could you?"

"How could I what?" I called down.

"How could you make that awful noise to such a tune?"

What was wrong with the tune? Then it dawned on me. *Red sails in the sun-set/ Way out on the sea/ Oh, carry my loved one. . . .*

"Oh no!" I gulped. How could I be so thoughtless? Malcolm! Her beloved lost Malcolm! "I'm so sorry, Mum," I called down. "Ever so sorry." But the damage was done. I knew she was down there crying. I couldn't go down to her.

The few times I saw Dad, he tried but couldn't hide his sadness.

That summer was unlike any other. Mum held a coming-home tea-party in the garden at which I danced for my aunts and cousins in my bare feet. I had my tonsils out, and the only bright spot about that was watching the arrival of the Earl of Athlone and Princess Alice at Pier One and seeing their royal procession pass below my hospital window in the Medical-Dental Building on Burrard Street. Perhaps the excitement was too much for me because the incision haemorrhaged right after that and didn't want to stop, keeping me in hospital for three more days. A week before the usual summer season opened at Pasley, I was sent there to spend those days with my cousin Con Bell-Irving and her fiance Rodney Browne. Her brother Ian and I shared the ridiculous honour of chaperoning them. Ian had a new record he played over and over again, especially when dusk was falling and the huge trees looked particularly black. It was called "Gloomy Sunday" and it was about someone contemplating suicide. Still in a soggy state of weakness, I became unbearably depressed.

For that whole summer I didn't swim or boat or run through the trails. The sun was too hot for me and I felt dizzy. I must have been allergic to the ether which was used in those days for tonsillectomies because the bitterness of it was on my skin for weeks. And although I felt wretched, I had to return to Vancouver several times to begin a series of electro-desiccation treatments for the warts on my hands. Over the next year this proved to be the answer to my problem.

As the season dragged by, conversations were sprinkled with comments about King Edward and his qualities as our new monarch. Mother spoke of him with affection and familiarity, reminding us that when he was Prince of Wales,

*Ascania*

he often used to come to Canada to visit his cattle holding, the EP Ranch near High River, Alberta, not far from her cousin's Virginia Ranch near Cochrane. She remembered dancing with him at a ball in Vancouver. Everyone thought he was splendidly sociable, not at all a snob. But she was not happy to hear of his present social gadding.

Soon it was time for me to return to England. In Montreal, the Sweeny cousins who called themselves my "Montreal Family" met me after the endlessly dull train ride from home. They took care of me elegantly for several days before putting me aboard the *Ascania*, sister ship to the *Ausonia*, for my third Atlantic crossing—tourist class this time. However, I had a few rather delicious evenings up in first class, dancing with the ship's officers, all of whom were properly trained for the ballroom. It must have surprised them that a kid of fourteen could follow so well. When we arrived at Surrey Docks, I got through customs and found a taxi to take me to Doffie's new address off the Brompton Road in Chelsea.

*First press photograph of Verity taken in London.*
*Aged sixteen. 1938.*

# 9
# ON MY OWN

The new cottage was comparatively modern—not more than a century old. Like Cheyne Cottage, it was set back between taller buildings on a narrow lane that led to the Brompton parish church. I can still visualize the small enamel plaque on the red brick wall of the building next to ours that gave the name of the lane, but I can't read the name, and bombs took the whole lane out in World War II. It used to run from Brompton Road along the railings that edged the cemetery which separated the oratory from the parish church. At the end of the lane a path led through a gate and across part of the cemetery to reach the parish church where my parents had been married during World War I.

While I had been gone that summer, Helen Taylor had moved in with Doffie. A well-built and well-corseted woman, she wore her hair short in a mannish cut. Her clothes were strictly tailored, grey or dark blue. The only cheerful bit of colour she allowed was a kerchief in a pocket or a bright scarf at the neck of a winter coat. She wore fine hosiery with patent leather pumps or leather tie shoes, no jewellery nor make-up but always kid gloves. Unlike Doffie's other friends, she didn't sing or paint or write and was as conscious of time as Doffie was immune to it. I could not understand why they were friends. She asked me if I would give her a nickname. The first thing I could think of was Skip, and Skip she was from then on.

To my embarrassment, the man-servant that the two of them had employed delivered my morning orange juice to me in bed, but since Skip was a working woman—that is, she had a job in a posh dress shop on Knightsbridge—breakfast itself, which he also prepared, was now served at a regular hour, which helped Doffie and me to set off early to dance school. However, he didn't last long. One day he just wasn't there and we managed without him. Doffie still insisted on delivering me to school by bus, and I continued to feel embarrassed and belittled by her overprotection.

During one of our early morning journeys, I enquired about visiting the Brompton parish church. Doffie encouraged me to attend and gave me several shillings toward the next week's collection. I began regular attendance at church, which permitted Doffie and Skip to sleep in without disturbance on Sunday mornings. If I arrived at church late and it was full, the verger welcomed me and gave me a kneeling hassock at the edge of the aisle. As a farewell gift from home, I'd been given a small, red-leather prayer book that had served me well with Miss Richardson. Because of her, I knew all the morning prayers by heart, the litany, psalms and hymns, but never having been confirmed, I sat quietly through Holy Communion. I loved the booming organ music and was carried away by the anthems. Here I begged God to forgive me for all my sins, for annoying Doffie, for sometimes hating her and for wishing I could be at home. Here I found expression for the sadness and love that seemed inappropriate with my aunt.

During the time I had been away in Vancouver, Miss Bedells had moved her school closer to Marble Arch, to Quex Road in Kilburn where she now had two studios. Her senior assistant remained Edna Slocombe, but in these enlarged premises she had also taken on other teachers. Although I was now well along with the RAD intermediate syllabus and the date for my examination wasn't far away, I was still considered a junior. Morning classes for the junior students were in the small studio with a new assistant. They included limbering and stretching plus a class or two with a teacher of national dance—depending on which professionals were teaching in London at the time—or Revived Greek dance, Dalcroix eurythmics or mime.

At one o'clock, after a bag lunch in the dressing room, we moved to the big studio for three solid hours of ballet.

First we worked through an elementary class with Edna Slocombe. This was followed immediately by the intermediate syllabus—sometimes checked by Phyllis. From four to five Phyllis instructed an advanced class with Edna's assistance.

The classes were large, twenty to twenty-five including the pupils. During centre practice, those students for whom the level of the instruction was designed worked nearest the front and got more attention. Taking an elementary class when I was an intermediate student made me look really good; taking an advanced class when I was only intermediate, I had to work like a fiend to keep up. But there would always be people better than I was, it seemed. Always.

I was now dancing with girls who were mostly older than myself, and though I loved every class, I sometimes became very tired. In addition, since I was never built to be a dancer, I had to work very hard to maintain turn-out. When I had begun, my shoulders seemed always to be up around my ears with my chin poked forward. It was necessary for me to create extra muscle to control my overly extended knees and minimize my sway back. As the exercises became longer and more complicated, getting to the end of each one often made me feel physically ill, but after a time I learned that those were the times to build muscle and gain stamina. In the long run I was lucky. We were all working far beyond the comfort area most of the time—that is, the small group of us who were determined to become professional—but dancers who get there too easily don't always stay up there, and what had been my weaknesses eventually became my strengths. Turn-out, which some would-be dancers come by effortlessly, can fail them—for instance, when descending from a jump—if they haven't the muscle to hold their landing position. And the same goes for the back muscles. In the end, my overly arched, weak back became powerfully strong, enabling me to land from high leaps without collapsing.

But as my studies got underway again, I saw less and less of the principal of this new and more elegant organization and missed the close relationship I had enjoyed with her. Then only a month into the term, Edna Slocombe left the school to go into partnership with an old friend from Liverpool, Sheilagh Elliott-Clarke. The new venture was to be a branch of Sheilagh's highly successful Liverpool "Studio School" where Edna herself had first studied. Together they opened a second professional school near Piccadilly, and for reasons unknown to me, I was transferred to their "Studio School." To my delight, so was my friend Phyllis Dakin as Piccadilly was easier to get to from her home in Bedford.

The students at the new London branch had the benefit of both partners' experience as each spent half of the week in London and the other half in Liverpool, with Edna teaching classical dance and the Revived Greek syllabus in both locations, and Sheilagh teaching modern dance, jazz, musical comedy, mime and character dance. Both branches thrived and the teaching staff had to be expanded to ease the load. As had been the case at Phyllis Bedells' school, the new partners hired several guest teachers, professionals temporarily living in London, who brought their special techniques and talents to the Studio School. Some could teach for a whole season, some for only a few weeks. For example, Sheilagh managed to get Buddy Bradley, a brilliant tap dancer and choreographer of that day, to teach us his American style of dance. The school employed two wonderful pianists who not only played for our lessons, but also accompanied those of us who made the competition finals, as well as our solo performances during senior classical examination. But the greatest plus of the Studio School was that Sheilagh believed in competition. She threw at us every creative idea that could possibly enhance our work and win prizes at the All England Dance Competitions, for which dancers came to London from dozens of qualifying heats and six rural semifinals.

Sheilagh Elliott-Clarke had already enjoyed a career that was a story of triumph, a combination of artistic entrepreneurship, spunk and unbelievably hard work. At a very young age, when her family was unable to support her theatrical ambitions, she had talked her neighbourhood friends into pooling their pennies until there was enough money for her to take one class at the local dance school in Liverpool. In return, she taught them everything she learned there. In this way Sheilagh began her own school, and staying one jump ahead of her pupils, managed to develop a unique style

*Verity, photographed by Aunt Doffie's friend,
Audrey Estob, in Chelsea, London. 1936.*

*Verity in her ballet frock after taking her intermediate exam at the Royal Academy of Dance. January 1937.*

as an actress, a mime, a song-and-dance performer and a jazz and tap dancer. Her primary interest, however, was to teach theatre and her reputation grew as did her school. She had already personally groomed world-class performers such as Moira Shearer and Frederic Franklin at the Liverpool branch. As the two Studio Schools became recognized, Sheilagh also took on the heavy responsibility of presidency of the Imperial Society of Teachers of Dancing for all of England.

Sheilagh was no sylph, but her sense of rhythm, her agility and her enormous enthusiasm overcame any doubt about her being a professional. With her dyed red hair and flashy earrings, her splendid red mouth and her probing eyes, her wit and her slashing tongue, she was a demanding and irresistible personality.

In comparison Edna Slocombe was slim and elegant, a quiet and lady-like person who, though she spoke gently, was also precise and a stickler for detail. For teaching she wore expensive, well-cut slacks and blouses that always looked new. Her hair never became untidy. During her last year as Miss Bedells' assistant, she had passed the final classical Royal Academy exam for advanced teachers. She was indeed a superb ballet teacher, who adhered to the RAD syllabi without wavering. From her we learned every turn and tip of head, every angle of shoulder. We learned the exact meaning of the French balletic terminology and were taught to recognize the basic musical structures that would be expected of us in our exams. She was exactly the right person to give me final coaching before my exam.

As a candidate for the RAD intermediate certificate, I was expected to have strong extensions, secure balance, fast foot-work, good *batterie*, to execute double *pirouettes* and show considerable elevation. *Pointe* work had begun at this level, but we were allowed *en pointe* only fifteen minutes per lesson. For my upcoming classical exam I would carry my blocked *pointe* shoes into the examination studio. I would wear a short ballet skirt, pink satin slippers and my very first pink silk tights. In those days the cost of real tights was far beyond the average student's pocket, so for us they came as separate stockings with seams that must be aligned straight from heel to buttocks and must under no circumstances be allowed to wrinkle. Although the knickers that would cover the tops of them had short tarlatan frills, they were minuscule. Dancers therefore used a method called "pennies and tapes" to keep the stockings up. The tops of the stockings were pulled up as high as possible (any excess length was stuffed into the crotch). Having made a loop with a slip knot at the end of a length of twill tape, one tightened the loop over a large English penny that one had pressed through from inside the top of the left stocking. Pulling upward, the tape was hooked over the right hip and across the back and down

*Verity curtseys to examiners following her advanced Royal Academy exam. February 1938.*

THE LUCKIEST GIRL IN THE WORLD

under the left buttock where it was attached to a penny at the back of the left stocking. Ditto for the right stocking. In other words, a pelvic straight jacket. It worked amazingly well and we got used to it, but it was a toss-up which hurt more, the bones in the bodices of our costumes, our *pointe* shoes or the pennies and tapes. I passed this exam with a mark in the eighties.

One grey morning less than a month after switching to the Studio School, I had been working with a group of advanced students in the big studio for an hour or so when I stopped to remove my woolly. I was so warm, in fact, that my tunic was sticking to me. Suddenly I noticed one of the mothers stand up and, looking at her watch, open a window. Leaning out, she listened to the roar of London's traffic. So did the other mothers. Within a moment we caught the feeling, stopped what we were doing and, remembering the day, went over to the open window. It must have been but a few minutes before eleven. Very soon I began to notice the lull as one upon another engine ceased to throb. Rather like going under water, there were sounds I could no longer hear. Taxi horns had gone silent. Busses had stopped. Cars, lorries, horse-drawn carts no longer moved. Not only in Piccadilly but everywhere, the air carried increasing quietness. No hawkers, no cyclists, no street musicians. But there was sound! Sitting on their window ledges, pigeons cooed. Starlings on the wires chattered. A horse shook his harness. I heard my own breath and a ringing in my own ears. Two minutes passed before Big Ben rang the chimes and the boom of guns on the embankment filled the silence. Still, no one moved. Four, five, six, seven, the solemn tribute continued, but now steeple bells joined in recognition, and Big Ben tolled eleven.

Gradually I became aware of engines re-started, wheels beginning to roll, gears changing upward, blurring the clear sound of bells. As the noise increased, it struck me how amazing it was that a whole city, a whole country, a whole empire could be brought to stillness with but one thought in mind. As usual I reminded myself that Uncle Roderick had been killed in the Great War and Uncle Mick had been dreadfully wounded, coming back to Vancouver minus a leg. But it was the sudden remembrance of Malcolm that brought home to me the reality of death. The world had stopped for all of

*Verity (2nd from left) at the Studio School of Dance rehearsing "Red Shoes" for the Pavlova Casket Competition. 1936.*

them. Suddenly I became aware of the cold on my damp tunic. We closed the windows and let ourselves become lost again in music and movement.

In order to gain professional experience, some of the senior students danced in nightclubs and cabarets. In late November 1936, the Studio School provided dancers for a floor show at Grosvenor House. I know I danced in some big, flowing number, waltzing circles in that huge ballroom, but I was distracted. Two years before in this very room, on his first leave from *Worcester*, Malcolm and I had enjoyed the charity party. Now, finally, I had to admit it. Malcolm was gone. Lost at sea.

Because of the high expectations Sheilagh and Edna held for their students and their insistence on professionalism, the Studio School became visible in all the competition classes including duets and groups. In a competition for the coveted Pavlova Casket, the group in which I danced won the famous trophy with a production of "The Red Shoes," long before the successful movie of that title featuring Moira Shearer. It was the first time the London branch had presented an actual ballet. Short but complete—about twelve minutes—it taught us about working together, telling a story together.

The plot revolves around a pair of enchanted red shoes belonging to a witch. With them she entices a little girl away from home into a life of theatrical brilliance and to an untimely death. Avril Jowett, the tiny child who played the waif and wore the red shoes, was only eleven but already an outstanding performer. She went on to star as Avril Navarre with the Sadler's Wells, later the Royal Ballet.

"Red Shoes" taught us how to build from simple, uncomplicated moves when we played and danced with our little friend, to the dramatic moment when the witch and the red shoes dragged her away from us. I was given the central position in the group because, according to my teachers, I was good at keeping the seven of us in close contact—even though we did not actually touch, we had to dance as a single unit. That compliment helped boost my morale, although it was already on the rise because my hands were beginning to improve. Obviously instructed by my parents, on my return to England Doffie had found the right doctor to continue treatment.

Meanwhile, all was not well at the house on Brompton Road. One morning, at the beginning of December 1936, Doffie had stopped me on my way to the bathroom. Without once meeting my eyes, she told me about a hostel that had been set up for out-of-town and overseas students of the Studio School. Edna Slocombe's friends, Mr. and Mrs. Wren, who had moved to London from Manchester, would run it and be the house parents. She thought it would be good for me to live there.

It came as a shock, even though I had become aware of a growing wall rising between me and Doffie and Skip. I really knew nothing about their activities, but assumed I was making life uncomfortable for their relationship.

"Whatever you say, Aunty." Though shaken, I wouldn't let on. "Would you still come and take me to school or could I manage alone? I'm sure I could."

"Yes, of course you can manage. I expect there will be other students coming and going from the school." She was so relieved she hardly left a breath between sentences. "Skip has a holiday coming up. She and I have been thinking of going to Portugal."

"Oh! Then will it be soon?"

"Quite soon. Next weekend, in fact."

And so I packed my trunk and my bags and went with

Aunty in a taxi to a big stone house on Holland Park Road. I met Mr. and Mrs. Wren and their two grown-up children—Betty, who had a job as a secretary, and Eric, who worked at Harrods, the poshest shop on Knightsbridge.

Neither of the Wrens was bird-like. Mrs. Wren was large and colourless, though bossy and opinionated. I'd say she wasn't very worldly-wise. In time I learned that she was also suspicious and vindictive. The old man, as everyone called him, was not in good physical shape and got pushed about by his wife, but he suffered without complaint. Mr. Wren had long since given up trying to be the man of the house.

Doffie stayed just long enough for tea, where the topic of the new king's ability to knuckle down and toe the line regarding protocol as applied to a monarch was discussed. Doffie and Skip had been more than a little interested in the gossip about the king's interest in modernizing the monarchy. I, like many other youngsters, had my own ideas about royalty and believed nothing could stand in the way of King Edward's coronation, but my optimism had been diminishing since it began to be rumoured that a certain Mrs. Wallis Warfield Simpson, an American, had asked for a divorce from her husband and the king had said he would marry her. The older Wrens were definitely not in favour of his marrying Wally.

Although there was next to nothing in the serious press, London's tabloids steamed with pros and cons much less polite than they had been in Canada. Wonderfully intimate articles about the forthcoming wedding leaked out. No, Wally's French wedding dress wouldn't be white; her blue two-piece sheath would be floor-length and have a high neck. Her undies would be of handmade lace. We commoners had taken a liking to Her Highness—it would be highness, wouldn't it?—and hoped against hope that the powers that were would find a way around tradition. But on Friday, December 11, 1936—just a week after I moved to Holland Park Road—my rejected and dejected hero told the Empire that he had chosen to abdicate in favour of the woman he loved. Edward would never wear the crown. He would be exiled forthwith, never to return. "Serves him right!" roared Mrs. Wren.

At the Wrens', I moved into a room with a blocked-up

fireplace and big bay window which suggested that the room had once been a lounge. I shared it with an older student called Peggy who wore a lot of make-up and stayed out late. Since I slept like a lump, she didn't disturb me when she came in, but I didn't like it that she sometimes smoked in our bedroom.

After Doffie left me at the Wrens', I remember feeling cut off—or was it cut loose?—from my childhood. But it was a subdued and saddened Doffie who finally came to visit me there several weeks later. She gave me an elaborately costumed Portuguese doll, a souvenir of her holiday with Skip, but after Portugal, Skip vanished from Doffie's life, and my aunt moved to an un-grand apartment in Fullham.

For as long as she had lived on her own, Doffie had spent capital whenever she could liquidate it—perhaps stocks and bonds that had matured. Though I knew nothing about money then, it comes to me now that, unlike the Scottish cousins who sailed oblivious through the continuing Depression years, Doffie was by that time in straitened circumstances, and the three years of expenses connected with my training must have put an even greater strain on her resources. From time to time Mrs. Wren made it obvious that Miss Sweeny owed her for my rent and board. Often Mrs. Wren told me she had been given no money for my tube fares or allowance.

Her physical disability, bronchitis and hectic lifestyle were fast aging Doffie, who must by that time have been close to fifty. As her energies and fortune waned, the rejection by Skip must have come as a huge defeat and soon, pathetically looking for a focus, Doffie once again became my doting aunt and I began to realize she needed me more than I needed her. Thus, although she had sent me off to live at the Wrens, Doffie now increased her interest in my work and often sat knitting on the studio window seat for long hours with "the mothers," an audience that was encouraged by the school.

To reach the studio from the Wrens' hostel on Holland Park Road, we students had to walk about half a mile to the underground station at Shepherd's Bush. After about fifteen minutes on the Inner Circle Route we changed trains at Oxford Circus and then took an escalator to the surface at

Piccadilly Circus. I remember the length and darkness of some of the tunnels where we passengers walked or ran like a river in flood. Hundreds upon hundreds of us. And I can still feel the piercing cold of foggy street air rushing down at us as we climbed the long, last concrete exit stairs, emerging opposite the grand entrance to the Regent Palace. There always seemed to be exotically dressed women hanging about near that door. I put my head down and walked swiftly by.

At the curve of Regent Street, where for centuries "The Goldsmiths and Silversmiths" have dazzled the world with truly beautiful tea sets and exquisite jewellery, a small one-way street which divides again within a hundred feet dips behind their pie-shaped building. This is Brewer Street. The Regent Palace Hotel stands between the south side of Brewer Street—once a street of breweries—and Piccadilly Circus. On the north side of Brewer, the Studio School of Dance had moved into the second and third floors of one of the old breweries.

Turning the corner onto this street, I had to walk in the middle of the road because too many vehicles were pulled up on its uneven sidewalks to do anything else. A little way along I would duck in between barrows and cars and head for the dark archway entrance to our building. Just inside on the right, grimy stained-glass windows on either side of a dark door with a little peephole in it gave gloomy hints of activity in what I learned was a nightclub. I never tried to see inside but went on to the end of the hall where our stairs began. Up six, turn. Up four, turn. Up eighteen. Slight illumination came from a window onto Brewer Street at the second floor landing, as well as from a shaded light which hung outside the door to the big studio. That landing (five feet by ten) served as an extra studio where a student having difficulty with an exercise was sent to work it out with someone who had managed to get the hang of it.

The next set of stairs led to a smaller studio on the top floor, which had a single dressing room and a loo with what was always referred to as a *wash-hand-basin*. Only once, but once was enough, alone upstairs, I opened the door to the loo and came face to face with a man waiting in ambush with his private parts exposed. I flew downstairs and told

Edna, who immediately phoned Scotland Yard. No one spoke of it again, but the upstairs door got a new lock, and we had to use a key from then on.

The heavy studio doors on each landing were painted brilliant green inside and out. The same paint had been used for the wooden window frames as well as for the ledge below the Brewer Street windows where the mothers and guardians sat to watch. From these windows I could look down on the backs of a pair or two of shining Clydesdales waiting with their wagons and hear the clatter and boom as barrels were unloaded and sent down chutes into basements. These windows also looked into the lesser back suites of the big old Regent Palace Hotel, and as we danced, we could watch window cleaners dangling in cages from the hotel. Sometimes I dreamed that I had a secret admirer in one of the bedrooms. This added considerable gusto to my performance.

The small lampshades that camouflaged the series of light bulbs hanging near the studio ceiling each wore a band of green and a band of maroon, and several wooden chairs had been painted to match. Our short silk tunics were maroon but the woollies around our shoulders were green, as were our leather practice shoes. Smart, I thought, and cheerful.

The only heat in our part of the building was provided by one small gas fireplace in each studio. Woollen tights and wrap-around jerseys kept our bodies from freezing, but in winter it took as long as half an hour to get feeling into my feet.

Sheilagh and her partner shared a little office against the wall opposite the grand piano in the larger of the two studios. In their washroom, which was a bit bigger than the one upstairs, they kept a few eating utensils on a shelf and a two-ringed electric burner. This is where the regular students like me produced meals, a week at a time, for the teachers and pianists who did individual coaching during meal breaks. For this we earned the odd private lesson.

My life at the Studio School was wonderfully full. Quickly bonding with my teachers, whose acceptance of me was something altogether new in my life, I respected their criticism which, though sometimes harsh, was positive, creative and encouraging. Sheilagh was a dynamic teacher who pulled out of me feelings I had been shy of and scared to express. Both teachers made me feel as though I belonged, unlike my impatient aunt who, understanding nothing of normal adolescence, had so regularly let me down, and my parents, whose child-rearing rules forbade the showering of praise or compliments on any of their children.

I fit happily into my new environment and felt free to respond to my teachers' enthusiasm with increasing amounts of my own. When it was my duty week, it gave me huge pleasure to dream up dainty lunches for my tireless teachers. Daily I shopped in Soho, an exotic district further along Brewer Street, where mobile barrows were loaded with edible delicacies from many countries. These lunches, however, were not always perfect. One day I got hell from Sheilagh for having peeled sections of pear for her. Grabbing a bite from the tray I'd put on the piano, she shot the fruit right into the piano strings, bringing her lesson to a halt.

I never tired of poking around in Soho, watching a vendor slice huge tomatoes with a gigantic knife at maniacal speed and put them into sandwiches with watercress, or sticking my nose into heavenly sweet bunches of wallflowers and violets. Oh, such violets! And I could buy two dozen peach carnations for a bob.

On learning that June 6, my birthday, was also Edna's, I wanted to give something special to my pristine and beautiful teacher—my friend since my first ballet lesson. I asked myself what I would like more than anything else to receive. Something elegant, beautiful—luxurious. I conjured up the picture of someone giving me an orchid. Oh, yes! That felt just about right, and I knew where I could get one. But when the time came to give it to her, I felt quite embarrassed. Wishing to hide my scarred hands, I almost flung the orchid at her and fled.

At the age that English people refer to as *ungainly*, I was one of the most awkward and tongue-tied of creatures but growing fast and on the verge of womanhood. One day, during a long, slow *adage* exercise, I felt a drop of sweat trickle from my scalp over my forehead and down the length of my nose. I flipped it off onto the floor as I felt a trickle down the back of my neck. From just beside my ears, drops ran along my chin before falling on my chest. They gathered in my eyebrows and fell into my eyes, stinging them, and from under my arms and in all my crevices, cooling rivers flowed.

When I could leave centre floor, I shook my dripping hair and wiped my hand across my face. I had no towel. I'd never needed one before. And when I looked in the small mirror over the fireplace, I saw that though my face was no longer scarlet, my burgundy tunic had gone black. All this happened during one lengthy exercise which I enjoyed enormously because I danced it so well, and from then on I couldn't wait to warm up at the beginning of class. Everything became easy as my pores opened.

Mrs. Wren didn't understand the change in me. I wanted a bath every night now, not just once or twice a week, and I used hot water to wash my tunic. She wouldn't listen as I desperately tried to explain my needs but kept telling me that if I didn't need hot water yesterday then I didn't need it today. We weren't getting along at all well anyway because of a recent bathroom episode.

Her daughter Betty had the only special bathroom privileges in the house: she was given priority in the use and ownership of the minuscule cabinet over the hand basin. This she stuffed so overly full that more often than not the metal door would not close. One weekend, having used the basin to wash my hands, I left the room, closing the door behind me. As it latched, I heard a crash. Returning, I found that a bottle belonging to Betty had fallen out of the cabinet. I picked it up, wedged it in under a shelf and managed to close the cabinet door. What I didn't see was thousands of hairline cracks spreading from the point of impact. At lunch, Mrs. Wren barked, "Who broke the sink in the bathroom?" No one answered. She prodded each of us. Still no one spoke up. I wondered who could have done such a thing. "Someone here did it," she charged, "and they'll pay for it!"

About mid-afternoon the realization struck me. The sink could have cracked when that bottle fell into it. I died inside but went straight to Mrs. Wren to tell her what had happened with Betty's bottle and to explain that I had not noticed anything at the time. I will never forget the look on her face when she told me I lied. "You knew all the time," she hissed at me. "I should have known it would be you!"

"But honestly, Mrs. Wren, I didn't see it then."

"You must have seen it, and you thought you could get away with it, you miserable liar." That hurt badly enough but she wasn't finished. "I can tell a liar to look at one. You have those thin lips. That's the sign—small mouth and thin lips. Never trust thin lips." I felt my eyes burn but I would not cry. I had not lied, but she crushed me with her thin lips description. From then on I loathed my small mouth and felt bitterly ashamed that my lips were not full.

This encounter did nothing for my self-esteem at a time when I already felt homely, unlovely and ill-prepared for womanhood. Stranded between my mother, who was unable to talk to me woman-to-woman, and my Aunt Doffie, with whom I was not brave enough to discuss intimate topics, I had no one to guide me. I had, of course, been told the basic facts of reproduction, although my introduction to the intricacies of human sex, years before, had been literally beyond my comprehension. That summer I was seven years old, and Dad had invited an old army companion to bring his wife and two children to Pasley Island for a weekend. The lad was between Sedley's and Malcolm's ages and the girl, Nancy, was ten.

Our cottage was small and primitive. Mum, Dad and the grown-ups slept indoors, but we children slept in tents, shacks, tree-houses or under the stars. My sister Moira and I usually slept in cots in the big tent behind the cottage where, above its raised wooden floor, an arrangement of layered canvasses was draped over a permanent two-by-four scaffolding and hooked down outside its four short walls.

By nine o'clock Moira was already asleep when Nancy, carrying an oil lamp, and I entered the tent to go to bed. Ready for sleep, I tucked myself into my cot. Nancy turned back her covers and blew out the lamp. I could hear her rustling about in her bed.

"It's cold," she said, and suddenly without any invitation she came to cuddle in beside me. "There, that'll be warmer, and we can talk without waking your kid sister." She wiggled down in my bed and pulled the covers over both our heads. "What do you know about making babies?" she whispered loudly in my ear.

From the moment of her arrival on the island, Nancy had been overpowering. Much bigger than I, she was bossy and opinionated and seemed to have no respect for her parents or mine. I was a bit in awe that she seemed interested in me, and before I knew it, I was following her around as a puppy might while she investigated my territory. Until now I had answered her questions willingly and even shown her my favoured climbing tree.

The unusual thing about her question was that she hadn't directly spoken the words, but spelled them out slowly, letter by letter.

"Nothing," I replied after finding my tongue. "Why?"

She went back to speaking. "Didn't your mother tell you?"

"Tell me what?"

"About how babies are made."

"Well, not exactly. Don't they...?"

"Listen, dummy, I'll spell it for you. Listen!" And she began a complicated story about Dad and Mum—so bizarre I knew she was telling fibs. With each item more impossible than the last, she spelled out:

"W H E N Y O U A R E O L D E R Y O U W I L L B L E E D B E T W E E N Y O U R L E G S. I F Y O U D O N T B L E E D B E T W E E N Y O U R L E G S B Y T H E T I M E Y O U A R E F O U R T E E N Y O U W I L L D I E."

Me? She was talking about me. Something must be wrong with her. "Whatever are you blabbing about?"

But she just went on spelling,

"W H E N Y O U R D A D W A N T S T O M A K E A B A B Y H E P U T S H I S T H I N G..."

"What thing?"

"You know, T H A T B I G T H I N G H E S G O T T O P E E W I T H I N S I D E Y O U R M U M S P E E H O L E A N D R U B S U P A N D D O W N U P A N D D O W N T I L L H E C O M E S."

"I don't believe a word you say. It's rubbish."

"It's not, I swear!"

"Oh, go away. Get into your own bed!" I literally kicked her out.

I soon fell asleep and by next day had forgotten the incident. It was only years later, when my mother finally decided it was time to tell me the facts of life, that it came back with a flash of shocking memory.

By that time our family was coming to the end of the

second bleak winter in the log cabin at Gibson's Landing. I was then almost eleven and having a bilious attack, and while the baby, Roger, slept and the others were at school, I lay alone and miserable in my attic bed. While I was in this vulnerable and subservient position, my mother chose to sit on the side of my bed, further pinning me down under the blankets, and in halting and evasive language told me the barest details about menstruation—known as "The Curse"— its beginning, purpose and end, and about intercourse. She told me she had to speak about it not only because I would be leaving home soon, but also because there had been gossip in the village about Mr. Darby's "poor behaviour" with the Smith girls. Not using any of the exact words, she tried to explain that when two married people loved each other it was permissible to do personal things that were not right at other times. There would come a day when one wished for children. The father would plant a seed in the mother's tummy where it would grow for nine months to become a baby. Then it would come out from between the mother's legs.

My head was swimming. It could not be true. Not my father. Not my mother. But it must be true. Nancy had told me the same impossible things. I couldn't look at my mother. I wanted to be sick, or cry. I turned my head away as she rose from beside me.

Without a touch or further word she left me there. I heard her go down the stairs. So this would one day happen to me, had happened to all mums and dads, was real! For a long time I looked at the stained roof and rafters, knowing every inch of them, feeding my pain into them. Then I told myself, "It's not for now." And I let sleep take me from my despair.

It was during my own fifteenth spring while spending a cold Easter holiday with Shum at Bankside that I began to study the women in my life more closely. I looked at Shum. How old was she? How old was Doffie? They must both be past having "The Curse," mustn't they? Anyway, neither of them had been married and that had something to do with it, hadn't it? No one around here to ask. Forget it!

But forget it I couldn't. One morning before the housemaid had lighted the fire in my bedroom, I awoke, and straightaway rising, took myself to the bathroom, a funny knowing in my head and heart that this was *it*. Quite calm and indeed delighted, I noticed the first warm red drop that heralded my maturity. I sat awhile thinking and feeling grown up, different.

It being early and the kitchen fire not yet stoked, I had to wash in cold water, and returning to my room, began to ponder how to cope. Fortunately, I had brought a good supply of handkerchiefs, as always washed and ironed by me. If I folded a couple of them to the right shape, they'd do, safety-pinned into one of my pairs of underpants. I felt secure and returned to bed to cogitate.

A little later Shum's housemaid, Bessie, knocked softly and entered, switching on a dim lamp. She brought me hot water for my basin and some kindling with which she lit a fire in the small grate. Taking a few pieces of coal from the bucket, she placed them carefully. Very soon they produced a friendly warmth.

"Thank you, Bessie," I said cheerily as she drew back the heavy curtains. Bessie, noticing my wide-awakeness, became chatty.

"They'll be otter huntin' this mornin', Miss. Did Mistress Anne lend you some breeks? It'll be a grand day, you'll see!" she said without waiting for my replies.

Good! I thought. I'll see Anne and James.

"Anythin' else, Miss?" she queried as she left the room.

"That will be all, thank you, Bessie," I said grandly to the closing door. I'd heard people speak to servants that way.

Yes, Anne Graham had lent me a pair of britches and a jacket. Anne was smaller than I, but these clothes were very bulgy—at one time they must have belonged to someone large like her cousin Mary. I put on an airtex shirt (I'd wheedled the money for it from J.J.) and a jersey, buttoned the breeks (I had added another handkerchief for good measure) and went down to breakfast. Cousin Shum came down in a jersey, tweed skirt, heavy stockings and bedroom slippers.

"Morning, Child!" she said loudly. "Have you Wellingtons? No? Well, maybe we can find you some." Nobody ever seemed to wait for answers to the questions they asked me. Perhaps I was too slow.

Breakfast was real porridge with cream, toast with marmalade, kippers and rice, all keeping hot on the side-

*The Dumfrieshire otter hounds getting the scent of the otter on the banks of the Tweed, from Shum Bell-Irving's photo album.*

board. I couldn't manage kippers, but stuffed myself on toast. Shum made a slurping noise as she drank tea. Her newspaper kept us from much talk, but she knew when I slipped away from the table.

"Be ready by ten. We'll pick up James and Anne on the way."

"I'll be ready, Cousin Shum. Thank you for a scrummy breakfast."

"You're welcome, Child." I sometimes wished she'd use my name. Returning to my room, I checked for damages and found, to my chagrin, that the curse was already through two of the three hankies. I was grateful to be able to burn the evidence. I put together several more kerchiefs and added another pair of panties, rebuttoned my britches and stuffed my jacket pockets in case of need, then descended the stairs to the entrance hall.

Shum, helping Bessie to pack a picnic basket in the scullery, pushed open the swing door shouting, "Come and try these boots! They're Bessie's. You like marmite, don't you? Better your boots be a bit big than too small."

It would be a long day, a very long day, but without concern I set off in high spirits, eager to rush along on foot with the crowd. I'd been otter hunting before and crashed through copses and coverts. The rubber boots were necessary because we would also wade out in the shallows of the river to be as close as possible to the otter hounds, those great, shaggy, lovable, howling beasts that knew their job. They'd snuffle about the river's edge, sometimes going after an otter in the river's flood, over waterfalls, all thirty of them full tilt, howling. What a sight! What a racket! All those hounds after one little otter, giving tongue with their mouths full of water. They sounded as though they were all drowning. It scared me at first, but not once I knew that they were having the greatest fun. So there we all were, crashing along, often over our boots, egging on the hounds. "Get him! Get him! Get him!" and "Go on! Go-o awnn!"

Although there were farmers and gentry and the gentry's children at these hunts, it was really a family affair. John Bell-Irving, Shum's brother, the squire of Whitehill (a third Bell-Irving holding on the Milk), was master of the Dumfriesshire packs of hounds—foxhounds, beagles, deerhounds and otter hounds. When John was away, Shum acted as master for all the packs, which meant a lot of travelling because each pack hunted the length and breadth of Dumfriesshire at one time of the year or another. Of course, there were several huntsmen for every pack who really did the work—care and feeding, breeding and training.

Sometimes Olly (if he was home from boarding school) and Teen would come otter hunting with Marda and their old nurse, Da. Even "the Black Aunts," J.J.'s two widowed sisters, Mary and Jessie, dressed in their trailing, ancient, voluminous black skirts, would be in it up to their bottoms and soaking wet! Olly would say of the Black Aunts, "They always wear those dresses. They pee standing up. They never wash."

*Shum Bell-Irving sidesaddle on Peter Pan,*
*stopping in a village while fox hunting. 1939.*

The meet that day was at Castle Milk, the Jardine family home. After the second draw—the hounds had lost the scent on the first one—and a fair run but no kill, we came back to where the cars were parked between the castle and a sweeping lawn. Here we halted for lunch, standing around eating marmite on white bread sandwiches and hard apples. The grown-ups drank something strong to warm themselves, sometimes giving a youngster a nip of it.

I wished there was a bathroom nearby. But no. The hounds were busy again on a scent. This time they'd get the bugger! Off we all went. But things weren't happy with me. For one thing I was chafed and sore. For another I began to fear there would soon be evidence of what was going on with me. I looked around for a place to hide. Straggling behind the field, I ducked into some woods away from the river and found a place out of sight where I could survey the damage. Boots off, I climbed out of Anne's britches and the two pairs of underpants, managed to concoct a new napkin from the contents of my pockets and dressed again, noting with relief that nothing, as yet, had discoloured those light brown breeks. Wellingtons on once more, I collected some rocks to cover my discards and scurried to catch up. Still sore but relieved, I rejoined my friends. No one asked where I had been.

The day wore on. I wished I could go home but my ordeal was far from over. I wasn't hollering anymore, although everyone else was. Another hour and another mile downstream, the whole mad dash came to a halt when the hounds sent the otter to ground. After the terriers went in to finish off the poor thing, we had to get back to the cars. Shum still had to deliver Anne and James home to Mossknowe. Then, of course, we must stay for drinks! What did the children want? Tea?

I had only one clean hankie left. Locking myself into the cold slit of a toilet off the vestibule I prayed, almost audibly, that I wasn't already a disgrace.

Still in luck, I managed to reorganize my problem. Then, holding my legs as close together as possible and taking very small steps, I crept back to the drawing room and leaned against an upright chair. Standing as near to the warm fire as they could get, everyone else was noisily reliving the day's hunt. (The kill later produced for me an otter's paw, set in silver, in honour of my having been there.)

When tea was over, Shum and I left for Bankside, and thankfully for me, we drove there via Lockerbie. Still confident that Shum knew nothing, I plucked up courage to ask her for money to buy something at the haberdashery. All she said was, "How much?" I didn't know, but guessed about five bob (shillings) which she handed me without comment. Hurrying as best I could into the shop, I returned hugely relieved, a brown paper package under my arm. For the next fifteen minutes I held myself on one cheek only, not pressing down on the seat, and flew without respect for Shum as soon as the car stopped at the top of her driveway. Clean and safe at last, changed into my dress-for-dinner skirt, I sauntered, trying to look as pain-free as possible, into Shum's fire-lit drawing room and sat bolt upright on a leather chair.

Who telephoned who first I can't guess, but Shum soon called me from the hall to say Aunty wanted to speak to me.

"Hello, Aunty!"

"Verity, my poor sweet. Are you all right?"

"I'm just fine, thank you. How are you, Aunty?"

"I mean, Shum told me about it. Are you really all right?"

"Oh, that. Yes, I'm quite fine, thank you."

"I'll be at St. Pancras to meet you on Sunday. You don't have to go to school if you don't feel like it."

"Don't worry about me, dearest Aunty. See you on Sunday."

Shum seemed quite hurt that I hadn't asked for her help but showed me, on our way to bed, where she kept her own supplies. Top right hand drawer of the chest in her bedroom, a room I had not entered before. "Never be afraid to ask if you need something, will you now?" she said, putting a hand on my shoulder.

*Shum Bell-Irving in her garden. 1939.*

When she picked me up at St. Pancras Station, Doffie was so solicitous about my wellbeing I didn't know what to think. It was as if I had been terribly ill or done something wonderful, and in that instant I stepped from one world into another, from my child's world to her adult one where she could speak to me as an equal.

Next day back at school, it was a bit embarrassing, but also rather delightful, when Edna suggested I take it easy if I didn't feel like doing turns. Doffie must have told her. "No," I said. "I'd rather keep on going, thanks." I did. And what's more, from that moment I became aware of a new limberness, a new ease of movement, an extra freedom in my body that continued to accompany my periods for all of my reproductive life. When other women complained of cramps, I never had any sympathy for them.

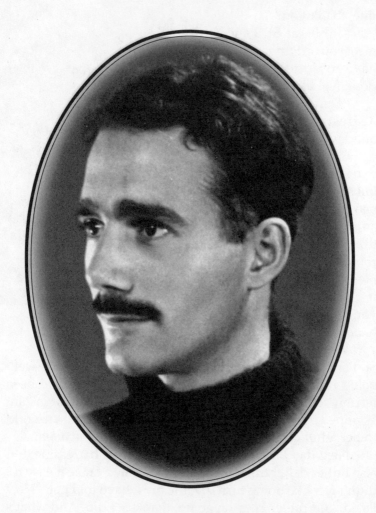

*Norman Benison Silk*

# 10
# NORMAN

*W*hen I first moved to the Wrens' in the fall of 1936, a thirteen-year-old dance student and her mother had two rooms on the third floor. More students came later, but at first there weren't enough of us to fill all the rooms, so Mrs. Wren encouraged Eric to bring a friend of his to board there. That friend, a lad of eighteen who also worked at Harrods, was Norman Benison Silk. Perhaps because I was the only other resident at a loose-end on Sundays, Norman and I took to walking the Wrens' Scotty dog, Mike, on those mornings. At first we headed for Kensington High Street and trod around Holland Park. This gave us a good stretch of the legs and we found enough paths and little hills to content us for several weeks. One day, Mike's pal, a terrier of sorts, joined us along the way and stayed with us till we dropped him off at home on our way back. This got to be a habit. Soon we had several regulars who were delighted to go with us on our longer routes to Kensington Gardens and even further afield. Eventually we had to ditch the dogs and take the bus. We knew we wouldn't be welcome in St. James's or Green Park with a collection of strays! After Mrs. Wren had fed us lunch, if the weather wasn't too awful, we'd give Mr. Wren a hand in the garden. Norman's strong back and arms were just what the old man needed to get his run-down garden into shape.

During the year and a half that we lived in the same house, my feelings about Norman only occasionally came to

*The romance between Verity Sweeny and Norman Silk lasted from 1937 to his death in 1944. Here, at home with his bagpipes. 1938.*

the surface. After the young dancer and her mother moved out of the top-floor suite, a girl of Norman's own age took one of their rooms. Being intensely involved with school, exams and competitions, with costume-making and going to theatrical performances, I had little time for romantic dreaming, so I couldn't understand the feeling of fury that came over me when he went upstairs some evenings to spend time with Ellen. Although I was invited to her room, I would not go. I struggled with my discomfort for a while, but since my Sunday walks with Norman continued, I soon forgot to be angry with him.

When I wasn't out or he upstairs, Norman usually spent the evenings with me in the living room. I sat on the floor by the coal fire, mending tights and sewing ribbons on *pointe* shoes. Norman didn't dance or know anything about it so far as I knew. "Schlew!" he'd exclaim through tightly clenched teeth, shaking his head slowly when I told him how many *pirouettes* I had done that day. Then he'd twinkle his dark eyes and the corners of his mouth would point up to the dimples in his cheeks. But though I noticed these things, in my naivete I failed to recognize this awareness as romantically sparked. He just happened to live in the same house and we had plenty to talk about, both of us being away from home and missing our families.

An intense feeling of his presence did attack me the day Norman decided to ask John, a new boarder on the top floor, to join us on our walk. I noticed how close beside Norman I walked, how nearly our hands touched, how much I wished John were not there and how silent I was while the two young men talked. I must have been holding myself tight, hardly breathing, for not only did I feel quite faint, but when we had walked only half as far as was customary for us, my bladder felt about to burst. I badly needed to find a public convenience, but I simply could not bring myself to tell Norman about my predicament, especially in front of John. I just had to hold on, hurting.

Something the same happened the first and only time Norman took me to a cinema. The sheer closeness of him overwhelmed me, and my head began to spin. All at once I got claustrophobic. Excusing myself, I fought my way from the best seat in the middle of the house to an aisle and rushed for some air. After I had found a washroom and cupped my hands to drink water, I could have gone back to my seat, but Norman was waiting near the exit and came to take my arm.

"Are you all right? Is there anything I can do?"

"No. I'm so sorry. I don't know what came over me. I just felt strange. Can we go home?" Norman held my elbow for the several blocks along Holland Park Avenue, gripping it tightly whenever we had to cross a street. It was only a short journey but I'll not forget that new and wonderful feeling of being cared for by someone special. I was aware of every breath I took as though I wasn't quite the same person. Perhaps I wasn't.

Doffie continued to plan my cultural education even though we no longer lived together, and when the date for the coronation of King George VI was set for May 12, 1937, she arranged for me to watch the procession. In their preparations for this event, the authorities in London were determined to avoid the dangerous overcrowding which had caused hundreds of accidents during George V's funeral procession. Barricades with gates were built wherever roads led

This ticket is issued on the condition that it is not resold.
Resale of the ticket will render it invalid.

THE CORONATION of THEIR MAJESTIES

KING GEORGE VI & QUEEN ELIZABETH

WEDNESDAY 12 MAY 1937

THE MALL STANDS

ADMIT ONE

| STAND | BLOCK | ROW | SEAT No. | PRICE |
|-------|-------|-----|----------|-------|
| 44 | C | G | 25 | 15/- |

*Verity's ticket to the Mall stands for the coronation of
King George VI and Queen Elizabeth on Wednesday, May 12, 1937.*

into the heart of the city—still a very large area—so that those who wanted to witness the coronation celebrations were obliged to find lodging or sleep in the parks inside the gates because they would be locked by ten o'clock the night before.

Although Doffie chose not to attend, she was able to get tickets through Canada House and bought me a seat in the stands built along the Mall. At nine-thirty on the evening of May 11 she took me by taxi to a friend's apartment inside the barricade. I was wearing the only smart thing I owned, a bright blue tweed suit that I had admired in a Wrexham shop window and which dear Cousin Marda had gone back to buy for me along with a white silk blouse. I must have worn my old but favourite blue suede shoes and some of those gorgeously sheer, pure silk stockings then available in London. And white gloves, of course.

To my surprise and delight I was collected at four the next morning by a familiar Canadian from Vancouver, a charming young man whose parents were friends of Dad and Mum. I knew who the Malkins were and I had seen

Bob, a pal of my brother Sedley, many times when we were children. Their summer place was on Bowen Island opposite Pasley. I hadn't dreamed such a handsome bit of luck could be mine, even for a few hours, and had a crush on him at once. But I knew from the start that a girl of my age, not yet fifteen with scars on her hands (not once did I remove my gloves), hadn't a chance with a fellow of nineteen.

The balmy spring night was waning, the floodlighting on the city buildings had grown pale, and dawn had begun to break as Bob and I set out through lamp-lit streets toward St. James's Park. People who had slept there were rousing. Others were already on the move to find places along the route. When we climbed to claim our seats—the best in the stands, I'm sure—we could watch the crowds gathering in dim light on the sidewalks below. Everything was orderly. We had loads of time. In fact, Bob suggested that since the day was sure to be long, we leave the stand and make a "reccy" to locate well-advertised washrooms in the park and find breakfast. And so we did, noting hundreds of military bandsmen and soldiers preparing to guard and entertain us. Returning from our feast of sticky buns and hot chocolate, we walked in leisurely fashion on the fine green grass between groups of people sitting and lying on rugs with bright cushions. Around the base of every tree they leaned or slept beneath leafy branches. Caught in this romantic atmosphere, strolling with a young man in the early light in London's heart, I savoured the beautiful and the good of that moment.

Then my eagerness not to miss anything made me pull Bob back up to our seats, from which we could see all the way down the Mall to the pale shape of Admiralty Arch. Looking west, although it was delicately hidden by overhanging foliage, we knew where the palace stood. From that direction would appear the royal coaches carrying their majesties and all the royal families in a joy-filled procession, although not for several hours yet.

The decorations were a wonder to behold. Each tall, tapered and curving lamp standard, alternating rhythmically with nurtured plane trees, supported an elaborate banner of purple and gold. As I remember them, the design on the elegantly tall banners was like filigree against the almost transparent fabric, catching the light when the sun rose, as did the streamers and little flags that shimmered and fluttered everywhere. As far down the Mall as we could see, the fronts of the massive stands were draped in light blue and had Royal insignia on them. It amazed me that such a huge job of decorating could have been accomplished in only a few weeks. It must have been planned many months, maybe years ahead.

At first the Mall was full of people walking, crossing over to find the best places, but those who had spent the night on the curb weren't about to move for anybody. Soon the police cleared the way, forcing the squatters to stand. Columns of soldiers in the dress uniforms of dozens of different regiments, hundreds and hundreds and hundreds of them, whose job it was to line the route from Buckingham Palace to Admiralty Arch, paraded into the broad Mall from stations where they had assembled in the parks. When they had taken up positions, they stood at ease and continued to stand without moving a foot for several hours. Then the whole guard was changed, platoon by platoon. The same thing must have been happening all along the route to the Abbey.

By seven in the morning not an empty seat remained in the stands, and every inch of pavement between the stands and the soldiers was jammed tight. Mounted police rode in pairs up and down the Mall. Military bands played in Green Park and in St. James's Park. With hours to wait before the coronation, a crystal-clear public address system began to describe the elements of the upcoming procession into which the royal parties would be amalgamated as it circled Buckingham Palace. We learned about preparations at the palace—whose coach was drawing up to receive its passengers, which famous coach horses would precede the Windsor Greys which always drew the State coach. It would pass, bearing the new king and queen, only twenty minutes before the coronation service was to begin. We were given historic information concerning other members of the royal family and explanations of their relationship to the crown, and as dignitaries entered Westminster Abbey, we heard what they were wearing and where they sat.

As the hour grew near and the May day warmed, the air seemed filled with music and excitement. There were several important participants in the event to look forward to, not the least of which were Canada's contributions. We learned that the largest ever contingent of North-West Mounted Police had travelled to London for this occasion. My mother had written me to watch for Uncle Duncan, Air Commodore A.D. Bell-Irving, who would march at the head of the Royal Canadian Air Force contingent. This was something of a miracle since Duncan had been seriously wounded in the leg while serving with the Royal Flying Corps during World War I. In fact, an ambulance stood by at the end of the route to take him to hospital. It wasn't necessary, however, and afterwards in a letter to Vancouver he described the coronation as "the greatest show on earth."

Dressed in scarlet, drummers and buglers, trumpeters and trombonists heralded contingents of Britain's army, naval and air forces in brilliant full dress uniforms. There were horses by the hundreds from many cavalry regiments and foot soldiers by the thousands, but I thought the great parade of Royal Navy was the best. It seemed to go on forever. Looking down on the ripple of white collars, dark uniforms sparkling with white webbing, they appeared to me very young and terribly precise. The way they handled the huge gun carriages—like toys, as though they weighed nothing—astonished me. Then came the blue, blue of the Royal Air Force. Grenadier Guards, Palace Guards and Household Cavalry created waves of magnificent uniforms and beautiful symmetry. But that was a mere beginning. Crowned heads, guests of the royal family, who had been arriving for weeks from every corner of the earth, rode in open landaus or on horses or they marched, according to their rank and station. And from every corner of the empire whole cavalry units and contingents of marching service men displayed unbelievable precision and even more unbelievable colours, particularly those of the Sikh and Gurkha mounted regiments. Of course, I thought the scarlet tunics of our Mounties and the perfectly matched black horses with checker-board patterns gleaming on their rumps were the most beautiful of all. There must have been a hundred of them. The crowd simply roared.

After we had listened to those parts of the service from Westminster Abbey that could be broadcast, we became part of the happy throng that flocked to Buckingham Palace to watch our new monarch and his family appear on the balcony time after time, as we all demanded one more and one more look at them.

Because the City of London had been caught badly unprepared for the immensity of crowds flocking to the funeral procession, the city government had almost overdone coronation safety precautions. People listened to the warnings and many chose to stay outside the heart of London. No one was trampled. Nothing frightening happened at all, and having been so intimately involved in that earlier royal drama, I felt a very slight disappointment in the orderliness of it all.

The most significant change in the Wrens' household came in late 1937. As a result of the Spanish Civil War, many refugees had come to London, among them the glamourous Angelicas, a whole family of dancers and performers, who moved into the Wrens' hostel. Suddenly the house was filled with laughter and music. Costumes hung everywhere and castanets sounded from the top floor down, especially in the one and only bathroom. Both Eric and Norman promptly found other digs. The next time I saw Norman he had joined the London Territorials, a reserve corps. He said he had no alternative while Europe was seething with the threat of war.

The Angelicas gave concerts in the living room. As I was able to play castanets quite acceptably by then, I joined in the fun. Of them all I could see that Chiquita, only seven but like a grown-up in a small body, sang and played the most brilliantly. She and her mother soon left the Wrens' because of Chiquita's need to attend regular school. Ysabelle, with the curvaceousness typical of Spanish dancers, had long, straight, black hair and fiery eyes. Sultry, but quietly dramatic, she and handsome Victor, small, dark and perfectly proportioned, were taken on by a London school to teach Spanish dance. The second sister, Dorianna, appeared to have contacts in London already. Her brown eyes and deep golden skin, combined with the richest of naturally blonde hair, made her a knockout. Ultimately, the father and two other sisters were "discovered" and booked into a night club in Soho, and from there went on tour. And so the boarders came and went.

As a dancer I was gradually becoming emotionally as well as technically mature, although it had been a slow and often difficult journey. During private lessons while Sheilagh and I choreographed the James Barrie character "Mary Rose" for an upcoming competition, I clearly recall Sheilagh pushing and pushing me till I cried over the plight of the girl I was portraying in dance. "I will gather twigs and light a fire for Simon. He will see it and return to the island to take me home." And at last as I danced and danced, I became Mary Rose—that fey child, that ever-hopeful, ever-trusting soul—and it felt wonderful. But when we paused, I noted with some embarrassment that Doffie, sitting on the cold windowsill, had also been crying. I must have touched some tender place in her.

At least twice a year for several days at a time I danced in heats, semi-finals and finals of All-England Competitions at the old Scala theatre. On those days Doffie would come to fetch me at the Wrens' in a cab. This was a necessity because I couldn't have managed on the underground. As well as my heavy make-up box, my basic luggage consisted of a case full of shoes and a big square box the depth of a short ballet skirt. In addition, depending on how many classes I had entered, there would be one or two bags of costumes.

Doffie fed me, too, since there was seldom time between classes for me to dress and go out, nor was there a restaurant near the theatre. Doffie would disappear periodically to find a pub where she could get a toddy to warm her inside and also buy "something on a bun" for me.

As well as having the support of a superb pianist for these competitions, one or other of the senior teachers would always turn up to watch our important classes. I remember on one occasion coming off stage in a semi-final and being met by Sheilagh. "What happened to your concentration?" she demanded. "Where were you?"

I shrugged. I hadn't been thrilled about this performance of Mary Rose, but I didn't think it had been all that bad.

"You let me down! You let the school down with that kind of unfocussed work. You'll no doubt reach the finals,

*Verity in her "Mary Rose" costume
photographed in Vancouver. 1939.*

but get off your behind and do some digging," Sheilagh said
with disgust. "I expect better from you." She left no room
for doubt that I had come to an impossibly useless time in
my life. But somewhere in there I sensed her faith in me and
I solemnly apologised. And yes, I did win with my final
performance after some further gruelling, almost brutally
demanding sessions with Sheilagh at night in the studio.
Time after time she brought me to tears before she was convinced I could truly feel and express the yearning and loneliness of Mary Rose. When at last I reached her with my
feelings, she took me in her arms and mopped my eyes.

In the autumn of 1937 Sheilagh prevailed on Edna's
sister, Marie Slocombe, an instructor at the Royal Academy
of Dramatic Art, to teach elocution and choral speech at the
Studio School part time. This opened more competitive venues

for the seniors, and the school name changed to the Studio School of Dance and Drama. I remember how those of us in the drama group huddled in winter by the small gas fireplace, reciting long, memorized speeches from Shakespeare. I was wrapped in an emerald green corduroy cloak that Doffie had produced to keep me warm between dance classes. This gorgeous, silk-lined, ankle-length cloak, fitted over the shoulders with a trim collar that fastened at the throat, did far more than just keep me warm. Over and over again it served to dignify or glamourize some character from whatever play we were studying. "Here, Verity, give Portia your cloak. Pick up the left corner with your right hand and toss it back over your left shoulder. No. Your right hand!" The cloak was used for dramatic effect by all of us.

It was thrilling to compete with the speech choir. Twelve of us, dressed in Tudor-style burgundy gowns, performed such works as "Congo Lament," "Tarantella," and "One Man Lost his Hat." And we brought home the medals. For this new form of competition, I recall making my own gown and helping several others. We worked until late at night with the materials spread out on the studio floor. Together we helped each other learn the rudiments of costume-making, a lesson of utter necessity. No money, no costume, no competition. Having danced all day, coached strugglers on the landing, fed the teachers, and sewed costumes by hand till all hours, I was dead weary when I went home to the Wrens' on the grimy underground. There, a dried-up dinner left on a plate in a warm oven was the most Mrs. Wren felt obliged to provide, despite the fact that hers was supposed to be a dancers' hostel. No one seemed the least interested in what or when we students ate. Not the teachers, not Doffie, not Mrs. Wren.

Although I didn't audition for it, I was one of the lucky students who, the following January, received a three-month choreographic scholarship from the Royal Academy. Once every week, twelve men and twelve women from various schools met for two hours of tuition. Our instructors were Ninette de Valois, classical repertoire; Frederick Ashton, contemporary choreography; and Ursula Moreton, music history. The material seemed to be away above my head, and at first I thought I would collapse from the rigour of the classes.

But I was stronger and brighter than I gave myself credit for being, and the excitement of gobbling all that new material simply added to my energy. I surprised myself by keeping up with the best of the students.

De Valois set exercises at a greater speed than I was accustomed to, but she detailed every move so clearly I had no problem remembering the intricate patterns. Expecting us to move on rapidly, she made few corrections. As for Freddy, he was not only embarrassingly sensual—addressing the women, he cupped his hands on his chest: "When you take *arabesque*, use these to weigh you down. That's what they're for!"—but he demanded things from us I had never dreamed a body could do. In fact, for him I happily threw myself onto my knees from a *tour jeté* and dragged the skin off the tops of my feet by running on my knees across the studio floor to pull up into a pleading gesture, only to rush back to do it again—and again. For weeks afterward my poor damaged feet wouldn't go into my red character boots. Ursula discussed music and filled my head with fascinating material, but I was glad we did not have to write an examination.

There were plenty of male dancers taking part in the choreographic scholarship classes, although they have ever been at a premium in the world of dance, and there were particularly few around the studios where I trained. But good, bad or indifferent, they seemed to get special encouragement and had assurance of professional careers so long as they had fairly good looks and could move with vigour.

I had first become acquainted with male dancers at Phyllis Bedells' school where a tall and heavily built young man attended intermediate and advanced ballet classes. His name was Christopher Cassen, and the only recommendation he came with was that he was Dame Sybil Thorndike's son. He had sandy hair and an excessive amount of exposed pale skin. When spinning or leaping, he splashed sweat all over the floor and whoever was nearby. Politeness prevented me from mentioning the acrid odour that always accompanied him, but I overheard several older girls in the dressing room giggling as they described the package of bath-salts and deodorants they planned to give him as a hint.

At the Studio School we had two boys in our classes. About my age, Graham Stark had slick black hair and a round face. He was a fairly good tap dancer and eventually made a career for himself as a comic. A couple of years older than me, Brian Blades was the right height to partner me in Fred Astaire's kind of dancing. We got along well and both understood Sheilagh's special style and daring as well as the intricacies of Buddy Bradley's tap choreography, but Brian was already getting calls for pantomimes and musicals and would soon be on his professional way.

Because of my interest in non-classical dance, Sheilagh decided I should enter the Song and Dance category of the next competitions, and Brian was assigned to coach me on a routine. Although I had enjoyed singing "Some day I'll find you, moonlight behind you" or "Petites fleures des bois" with Doffie and her crowd, Sheilagh chose the flashy song "You-oo-oo-oo! Gee, but you're wonderful, you-oo-oo, lovely you." And lo and behold, I learned it! Fortunately, the competition only required one chorus of vocal plus a chorus and a half of dance, and Brian warned me, "You'll have to shout it—bellow it out—or no one will hear you." So with my now terribly proper English accent, that's what I did.

The number began with an erratic and syncopated entrance—ta, ta ta, ta ta, .. ta ta, ta ta .. ta .. ta .. —as though my feet could hardly keep up with my body as it flew from the wings to centre stage where I slapped my tap shoes wide apart and spread my arms to the audience. In rehearsal, in rhythm and on pitch, I jazzed my way through the lyrics with appropriate gestures, with flashing eyes and all the confidence I could muster.

Just to think that you love me,
Makes my future look grand.
I swear by stars up above me,
I'm darned if I don't,
Feel like writing a song,
A song about you-oo-oo-oo,
Music and words about you-oo-oo,
Lovely you.

And there the dance began. It included nothing terribly complicated tap-wise, but all the moves covered territory and were unexpectedly peppered with claps, heel beats, high kicks and quick spins. I used my head and eyes and my arms and hands to accentuate every beat, and finished with a wide circle of tapping spins that, having brought me back to centre stage, gave me the perfect opportunity to repeat the slapdash, erratic rhythm to exit opposite my entrance as though falling into the wings.

I wasn't a musical comedy singer, but the vocal was short and I did the best I could with it. The dance was a treat to do, and as long as I was rehearsing in the studio, I had great confidence. For a costume, Edna came up with her own slimfitting navy-blue slacks and a white shirt with a midshipman collar. My tap shoes were fairly new and shiny black with sharp bows on them.

The day came, and in the dressing room at the theatre Edna gave me a glamourous face. She undid the curlers she had put on top of my head, back-combed and poofed the front bit, slicking the rest of it back with a lot of sticky goo. When I was dressed, I went out front and watched the whole of the class before mine, but sitting there in the darkness, I began to notice that my teeth were chattering and my heels were hitting the floor and bouncing up again and I couldn't stop my knees from actually knocking together. Did I doubt my ability to shine in this unfamiliar style? Was I just so excited I couldn't sit still? I have no idea.

After the winners were announced and my class called, I went backstage to warm up. I wiggled my ankles, rolled my shoulders, and took some deep breaths. There were at least six contestants before my turn came. When it did, I clattered across the stage; Ta, ta Ta, ta Ta Ta, ta Ta, in a reckless mood. Somehow I remembered the words and gestures and got them out brassily, but what came next I haven't the slightest recollection. I guess I did the whole thing, but with an increasing roar in my ears and with everything around me going black and blurry. When I staggered off... off... off into the wings, I collapsed on the floor. Someone brought a chair and sat me on it, shoving my head between my quaking knees. My teeth rattled audibly. I gasped for air and dripped sweat, but with a friendly hand to support me and a glass of water, I recovered enough to creep away to a seat high up at the back of the gallery where I could watch the finish of my class.

After a pause for the judges to sign the certificates, I heard "Musical Comedy, Song and Dance, class three, number seven, Verity Sweeny from the Studio School of Dance and Drama. . . ." I thought I was being politely excused but he continued, ". . . is in first place and has been awarded the silver medal. Congratulations, Verity!" Astonishment was my first reaction, then amazement when I realized that my body must have done it without my brain. I scrambled out of the gallery and down the back stairs. "Where is she?" the judge called. "Will Verity Sweeny please come on stage to accept her certificate?" Breathless, I staggered out onto the stage and took an embarrassed bow.

*Verity in publicity photo by Artona in Vancouver. 1939*

# 11
## Going Home

Although I did not understand the brinkmanship of world politics being played out during the spring and summer of 1938, I could not avoid the sombre atmosphere in Britain. Like a sickly cloud it descended on everything and everyone, signalling the end of an opulent era. Optimistic as the government tried to be, and hopeful as Doffie and her friends appeared to be about a settlement with Hitler, there were indications all around us of preparations for the worst. In every chemist shop window, displays of gas masks and information about how to use them in a gas attack left no doubt about the possibility of war.

During that spring Norman still occasionally joined me for Sunday walks or came to have tea with the Wrens, but with my gruelling schedule and dates coming up for both my Imperial Society exams in modern ballet, Greek, musical comedy and tap and the advanced certification from the Royal Academy in classical ballet, I saw less and less of him. I learned he had quit his job at Harrods and transferred from the London Territorials, a home guard militia, to the kilted fighting regiment, the London Scottish.

I saw Cousin Ian Maitland for the last time during the spring of 1938 when the Lady Sylvia Gwendolin Eva Maitland, daughter of the Earl and Countess of Lauderdale, married the sixth Baron Carew. I had never been to a wedding and was excited to be asked, although the invitation had come to me only because Sylvia's Aunt Marda was my cousin and good friend.

Marda must have been in cahoots with Doffie because Doffie's friends collected cast-off clothing from which I could create an outfit to wear to the event. Not yet sixteen, still gangly and awkward, I'd had no opportunity to develop a taste in clothes, so I leapt with delight at the conglomeration of ridiculous junk Doffie brought to Holland Park Road. I chose a dark, short-sleeved, calf-length, silk print dress as the base. Over it I slipped a brown shantung redingote. "Not bad!" This open-down-the-front, buttonless coat, which fell below the hem of the dress by about five inches, had long, loose sleeves. On my head I put a lacy, brown, broad-brimmed hat with flowers on it. To all this I added blue-and-white, spike-heeled sandals bought in Soho. I also owned long white kid gloves which I pushed up under the coat sleeves. Make-up? I would wear plenty. Because of their perfume, I bought myself a corsage of yellow freesias. I cringe to think how I must have looked in what I thought was a glamourous outfit.

Since Marda was involved in the wedding party—Teen was to be a bridesmaid and the twins pageboys—when the day came, she sent a car for me. As I entered the church—St. Margaret's Westminster, London's most fashionable church—someone took my invitation and ushered me to a pew. Among that enormous crowd of strangers, I witnessed the elaborate wedding ceremony in solitude.

Afterwards, someone took me to the reception on Knightsbridge Avenue. It was held in two huge old row houses that had been joined together by knocking out walls between reception rooms. The lobby where we entered was already filled to capacity. There, whoever delivered me vanished, leaving me quite alone in the throng. But from somewhere across the room Poop saw me and pushed his way through many bodies to stand beside me. Gradually we moved toward the base of a grand staircase where Poop let me go ahead, and we followed the flow of guests at a snail's pace up toward a gallery. As I hung onto the wrought iron bannister, a posh young woman turned and looked down at me.

"Are you related to the bride?" she enquired. Noting a certain iciness in her expression—one I had learned to know quite well—I pulled my small self to full height and answered, "My grand-father and Sylvia's grandfather are first cousins. Are you related?" She lifted her chin and moved up a step.

Crossing the gallery at the head of the stairs, we entered a vast room of glittering chandeliers and mirrors where the reception line actually began. The butler asked my name, which he then repeated loudly. With Poop close behind me, I said polite how-do-you-dos to dozens of unfamiliar people who all knew Poop although they called him Maurice or Major. The reception line continued through an archway into a second equally vast room,

*Maureen "Teen" Ormrod with her twin brothers, James and John, dressed as attendants for the wedding of Lady Sylvia Maitland to Lord Gerald Carew at St. Margaret's, Westminster, London. 1938.*

where I began to recognize Bell-Irvings and Jardines and finally Maitlands. And there, as I knew he would be, was Cousin Ian, the father of the bride. But this time he was no threat to me. I looked him straight in the eye and passed by. I kissed Sylvia and shook the groom's hand because that's what everyone else did. Sylvia didn't seem to know me. I don't remember seeing Marda or the twins, but I remember grinning at Teen. With Poop still behind me, I left the room. Re-crossing the gallery, we descended another grand staircase into another lobby. Ahead was an open door leading out onto Knightsbridge. I accepted Poop's offer to take me home in one of the waiting taxicabs. We rode almost wordlessly through London's streets.

*So that's a wedding!* I said to myself, my thoughts ranging from awe at all the elegance to bewilderment. *What happiness could Sylvia possibly find among all those stiff people?*

In the grip of a London heat wave during June 1938, among a select group of keen dancers, I attended my first ever summer school. Doffie sat on the window seat with the other silent watchers. Behind them, every window was wide open. With Edna setting the pace, we students had been pushing ourselves to the maximum for over an hour and now stood where we had been working, spread across the studio, taking deep breaths and mopping sweat. I wasn't the least tired. In fact, I had never felt so capable, so strong and smooth. Nor had I felt such energy as was flowing through me. My exhilaration came from a new realization. I was not just good, I was damned good!

It was during the next long *adage* exercise, beginning with the unfolding and high extension of my left leg to the side *développé à la seconde ecarté* arms opening wide, that I felt the sweet thrill of being perfectly secure. I then executed another extension *développé devant à quatrième*, arms in *attitude devant*. Next, while my supporting leg pivoted—little rises inching the heel forward—I carried my working leg high beside me for a half turn. Carefully tracing in slow motion the shape of what would ultimately become a whipped turn with two high springs, I took four slow counts to move my left arm to high fifth position, then opened both arms as I continued to turn my body away from my high working leg, noting with pleasure the easy rotation in my hip socket. On completion of the full turn I gently placed my arms into *arabesque*. My eyes in line with my front arm, I held the position steady as a rock.

Aware of the spaces all around me, I knew that my body was perfectly aligned. It was during the slightly faster second section, where rises replaced the pivots, that I realized I had total control of my body. I didn't have to pull up— I was up! I could hold the rises without wobbling and whip the turn into *arabesque* with ease, holding steady at the end on a bent knee. After all these years my muscles had finally become strong enough to obey the merest messages I sent to them. Suddenly aware of having arrived at a plateau, I glanced at my audience and realized they had become aware too. Some great self-assurance had arrived in my work, and recognizing it, the watchers were giving me their undivided attention. Part three, an exercise done with springs, was an expression of sheer joy. I had never before felt such power and control.

When we finished, I looked at Doffie. Tears were running down her face as they were down mine. I felt her joy for me, but deeper still I felt the sadness in her little body. I had done something she could not do. While she wept with joy that I had achieved a plateau and could from here on chase perfection, she must also have mourned her own blighted artistic career.

As the threat of war grew, my parents' letters began to be filled with their anxieties about my safety, and they urged me to come home. Sheilagh and Edna, however, wanted me to complete my advanced exam and even have a try at Solo Seal before leaving England. Finally, on my parents' orders, Doffie booked passage for me at the end of July, a date which would allow me to complete my examination schedule.

The Royal Academy advanced level demands total suppleness, high, strong extensions and a wide range of *pirouettes*. It also calls for slow, strong and liquid carriage of legs and arms in *adage*. Footwork must be brilliant and the student must execute high leaps of many varieties, landing lightly and quietly. *Pointe* shoes are worn for the entire centre practice. Full balletic dress with appropriate hairstyle is expected.

My exam was a gruelling ordeal under the critical eyes of three ballerinas—each a "Prima Ballerina Assoluta" in her time—Russian Tamara Karsavina, Danish/British Adeline Genée and Britain's own Phyllis Bedells—plus three more Royal Academy adjudicators. They were kind to me and I passed. I would have liked an honours certificate, but I value the one on which they signed their names.

Although few students can afford to stay in school long enough to accomplish it—most are already struggling as professionals—a further Royal Academy examination called the Solo Seal can be taken by purely classical dancers aiming for solo roles in a company. It demands expertise in performing unseen material—as much as sixty-four bars of new choreography—as well as an original character piece arranged by the student, up to three minutes in length. It also demands a considerable amount of poise and self-assurance. Few dancers pass this on their first try and I took comfort in this fact when I failed in my attempt. At least the adjudicators commented favourably on my own choreography, an emotional piece called "There once was a peasant with a field" or "Drought." Here I was in my element.

Meanwhile, Doffie had been making a real effort to bring my wardrobe up to date. Was it to impress my parents that she bought me a gorgeous pale green suit with an angora jumper of pure periwinkle? Had someone told her that since I was growing up I needed to dress like an adult? In only a couple of short shopping trips, I acquired a dark green duffle coat, fresh undies, stockings, both navy-blue and brown-and-white spectator pumps, a slim, slit-at-the-side linen sheath, gloves and a summer purse. Doffie said it was long overdue.

Close to departure day, she arranged with old Mrs. Hamersley's daughter, Tiny Oliphant, to take me to her home north of London for a day or two, see that I was properly packed, then drive me to Liverpool from where the *Duchess of Richmond* would depart for Montreal. The evening before leaving the Wrens', I was cleaning my room and packing last belongings when Betty Wren called me to come upstairs for a cup of tea. I was wearing an old skirt and jumper, but up I went. Norman had arrived and was already in the dining room. He greeted me with, "Well, Sweeny. So you're off to Canada, are you?"

"Yes, I leave here tomorrow."

"So I've been told. You must look forward to seeing your family."

"Oh, I do. It has been a very long time." Mrs. Wren offered tea and scones, and Betty asked Norman about his activities with the London Scottish. I learned that he was going on manoeuvres very soon and listened while they discussed the probability of war. But we had only been sitting at the table for ten minutes when Norman suddenly pushed his chair back.

"Well, I'll have to be going," he said. "Goodbye, Sweeny." And without further farewells he departed. Flying down the stairs, he opened the front door noisily and closed it after him with a bang.

For a moment no one spoke, then I asked, "What's wrong with Norman?"

To which Betty replied, "Don't you know?"

"Know what?" said I impatiently.

"Didn't you know? He's dotty about you. He always has been."

I hadn't understood that he had only come to say goodbye to me. I wanted to

*Norman Benison Silk with the London Scottish Regiment. 1938.*

hide and quickly excused myself to finish packing. Lying awake that night, I wondered what I should have said, how I should have behaved if I'd had any inkling of his feelings toward me.

There were no long goodbyes next morning when I left the Wrens', no hugs or kisses. I was going home at last and wanted to be on my way. Tiny collected me and my assortment of bags at around eleven and drove me first to Aunty's flat, where a lunch tray waited on a table by a small fire. Aunty cried. She knew far better than I how long it might be before we could meet again, and she knew how fragile our relationship remained. I felt very sorry for her loneliness.

It was a relief to be on my way again with Tiny. I didn't know her well, but I did know that she was one of my mother's oldest and best-loved friends. During those few days in an unfamiliar setting, and especially at night, I churned over many questions. How would it feel to be at home? How would I fit in with my family? Who else would I know? What would happen to my dance career? I remember a strange sensation in my throat, a taste that I could only describe as pink, that wouldn't swallow away. I felt tiredness settling on me, and sadness.

Tiny didn't fuss or ask questions. She washed and brushed my hair. She produced a wonderful old cabin trunk—bound with bamboo and with stickers on it from places in the Middle East—which took care of everything I owned. She showed me how to pack properly and labelled even my handbag for the long journey. Then, taking a picnic basket with us in her comfortable car, we set off for Liverpool, a drive of about seven hours. It was dusk when we arrived at dockside. A customs officer stamped the trunk and a porter took it away. We went aboard into the "smell of ship" and a steward took us to my small cabin on D deck. He opened the white-painted metal door and stood back to let us enter. To my utter amazement there were not one but three bouquets of flowers, one from Doffie and two from Norman. Tiny only stayed a moment, then left with a cheery "Bon Voyage." I was alone.

I had been told what to expect of the Irish Sea, and it lived up to its blustery reputation, but I wasn't expecting to be slowed by fog and to see icebergs as we crossed the North Atlantic. Thoroughly warm in my new duffle coat, I spent hours leaning on the rail, feeling the chill on my face and absorbing the blue-green atmosphere. Around me, other passengers shouted to hear their voices echo from the ice surfaces. Entering the St. Lawrence, the weather changed dramatically and so did the way we had to dress. Visible heat waves seemed to come at us, distorting shapes and distances. Passing under bridges on our way inland, I could have sworn the ship would hit them, a most unnerving feeling. August in Quebec was hotter than anything I had experienced before. When my Montreal family collected me from the ship, I was glad they said we'd be driving directly to their cottage in the Laurentian Mountains. Dreaming of cooling off in mountain lakes, I was shocked to plunge into hot water! However, dramatic thunderstorms every hour or so kept the air fresh, and gin sours—made with lake ice stored from the last winter—added to my festive, home-going mood.

In Vancouver, my tall, wonderful Dad stood on the platform in his "greyers" and navy blazer with the white shirt and navy-blue polka-dot bow tie I so well remembered. "Dear thing," he said, taking both my hands. "How good it is to have you home." Never physically effusive, the years of separation had added to our formality.

"And good it is to be here at last," I replied, holding tight to his warm hands and looking into his scrunched-up blue eyes. "I have missed you all so very much."

He carried my small bag, collected my trunk, then drove us to the North Vancouver Ferry in the Green Misery. Like old times, we both did our "I-think-I-can-I-think-I-can-I-hope-I-can-I-know-I-can!" routine, urging the old car up the steep slopes of Lonsdale, turning off at Kings. I was nearly home.

Mum had come back to the city from Pasley Island to be there, waiting for me. This time when she hugged me, I knew it was for me—not Malcolm. Dad only stayed a few minutes. Though I wasn't aware of it, he already held a reserve commission in the Seaforth Highland regiment and was preoccupied with exams to become an active service artillery officer.

I went through every room in the house and out to the back where I'd made a garden the summer of 1936. I looked to see if the tree-house was still there. It was. And so was the old chicken house Moira and I had painted with huge nasturtiums. Mum said that before taking off for Pasley, I could if I chose attend a luncheon at the home of her friend Mrs. Swan—to which we had both been invited—and a garden party for young people—at which I could wear my new sheath. They both sounded divine.

I shocked Mum by accepting a sherry at Mrs. Swan's, but although I swished around at the garden party trying to feel important and glamourous among my contemporaries, the sheath was uncomfortably tight and I hardly recognized anybody. It was far more interesting to don shorts and climb aboard Mack's old *Tymac*, a water taxi based at the foot of Columbia Street that delivered food and visitors to Pasley. I could smell the moss as we rounded Roger Curtis Point and came in sight of our family's island.

We were well into a summer that had been very dry. The meadow was yellow and the roses around the vegetable garden nearly over. Crickets sang and everyone looked tanned. I borrowed a bathing suit from Moira and swam in the clear, warm sea. Here I knew almost everyone and everyone seemed glad I had come home.

September called my cousins and friends back to school while I checked out all the local dance teachers except one. This particular woman, an American named June Roper, was reported to have used students from all the Vancouver schools for a successful Junior League production and then stolen the best dancers for her new B.C. Ballet School. I decided that ethically I should have nothing to do with her.

After I had wasted several months puttering from one studio to another, my dear Aunt Bea Abercrombie, now separated from her husband and living in a quite charming boarding house in the West End, took charge once again. She convinced my parents they must find some way to finance a room for me in the boarding house where she lived so that I could attend June Roper's school. In the afternoons I cleaned silver at Carmichael's, a silver shop on Howe Street which Bea managed. For this, Bea paid me just enough to cover my fees for the morning professional class at B.C. Ballet School. I quickly realized June was an extraordinarily talented person and a demanding teacher.

From the senior students at B.C. Ballet School I learned about serious dieting and immediately joined the grapefruit league. I began the routine of self-regulated practice between seven in the morning and the invigorating professional class at eleven. In those early morning hours, students shared experiences—technical skills and some obvious tricks to gain more control of balance *en pointe* as well as perform multi-multi *pirouettes*. I had much to learn from their western training and was glad of it. In return I explained what I knew of body alignment and fluid style, which they asked me to demonstrate.

In November 1938, at home in the house in North Vancouver, Dad asked if I would like to attend the New Year's

Eve ball at the splendid new Seaforth Armoury. What young girl wouldn't? Mum explained that guests would be expected to dance Scottish reels to a pipe band and that rehearsals would take place at my cousin Budge Bell-Irving's house. Consequently, on several occasions after my dance classes, I took a bus to the home of Budge, a Seaforth officer, and his wife Nancy. The three of us and a young man from the regiment pushed back a sofa in their living room so that Budge could direct us in Scottish dances. I enjoyed showing off.

Mum offered to make me a gown—actually to add a fresh skirt to the ivory-coloured Maltese lace bodice she had worn as a debutante. *That old thing?* But then she showed me the pearl-embroidered waistband from her wedding dress—designed with a sunburst and a waterfall of pearls at the bosom—which, she explained, she would use to cover the join between the lace bodice and the new, full, ivory taffeta skirt. The pearl band looked old but was in excellent condition. I didn't think Mum's eyes were strong enough to sew all of this together, but I figured I could help if necessary.

On the morning of the party I had my hair done at a small shop near home, and that evening Dad delivered me and my large cardboard box of clothing—which now included cream-coloured shoes, long white gloves, Great-granny Bell-Irving's McBean tartan sash and her wedding bracelet, a cairngorm brooch to hold the sash, a short brocade cloak fashioned out of Granny's wedding cloak, make-up, as well as my quite gorgeous dress—to the Bell-Irvings' house. While I was dressing, Nancy brought me a corsage that had just arrived—three perfect white camellias from Mum and Dad. By then I should have guessed what was up, but I didn't.

Budge in his Seaforth *trews* and scarlet tunic and Nancy wearing a MacKenzie sash over an elegant gown of cream satin were a regal pair. Budge drove us to the armoury and there my own Dad in full evening dress took my arm. (My mother had ceased attending big social events of any kind after Malcolm's death.) Even then I didn't know that he belonged to the regiment. Dad provided a dance programme for my wrist and, having written his own name for the first and last dances, introduced me to a coterie of subalterns who each asked for the honour of a dance with me. I met several other young women, all in white gowns; two had been at school with me when I was seven. I'd never seen my cousin Con dressed up before, but there she was, stunning in a gown of royal purple.

Dad escorted me to dinner, after which all the young ladies retired to the powder room for a final check of coiffure and make-up. It was then, to my surprise, I learned that they were debutantes and about to be presented to the lieutenant-governor, the Right Honourable Eric Hamber and Mrs. Hamber, and that I too was a debutante. I was even more surprised to discover, when Dad presented me, that he and the Hambers were long-time friends.

After the parade and hand shaking came the Scottish reels. Each girl had a dashing young officer as her partner. It was evident that everybody had practised, including Mr. and Mrs. Hamber. It was huge fun dancing to the pipers with everyone laughing and talking, although in the midst of it I burst the stitching where the ends of the pearl girdle met at the back and had to be safety-pinned. But that was the only slight disaster of the evening. My hair behaved. My make-up stayed blemish free. How could I be so blessed? But the best was still to come.

When a ballroom orchestra replaced the pipers, Dad came to claim the first dance. To my utter amazement, he not only danced, but danced divinely. He didn't look at me or speak, but guiding me carefully, swept me across the floor whenever a space cleared and reversed us out of difficulty when the floor seemed full. He was the smoothest partner I'd ever danced with. I think he too must have felt the thrill of it.

A last waltz with Dad signalled the party's end. He whispered that he had picked up my street clothes and had a rug ready in the car to keep me warm. We said our thank-yous and farewells and went home together in the old Green Misery. Mum awaited us with such a twinkle in her eye. "Did you have any fun, you two?" Turning to give me a hug, she said, "You look as fresh as a flower. Were you the Belle of the Ball?"

"She certainly was, my dear," said my father.

"Oh Mum, you should have been there. Dad is the best dancer in all the world. And you didn't tell me! You didn't tell me anything!"

*Verity in Polish dance costume in Hollywood. 1940.*

But in the midst of my pleasure, I was aware that once again they had made a decision in my life, as lovingly as they were able, but without consulting me. I realized how often I had needed the closeness of family and been denied it, and I knew that even now, although physically returned to my family, I was not part of it. After five years adrift, there was no anchor for me here. But I knew at last that I really was the luckiest girl in the world because I was free to fly.

*Verity Sweeny joins the Canadian Army Show. Canadian Women's Army Corps, Ste. Mary's Priory CWAC Barracks, Vancouver, 1943.*

# EPILOGUE

*I*n the spring of 1939 June Roper advised a group of us to head for California. Study with Bronislava Nijinska was her suggestion for me, and that is what I did until Dad's sudden death in a military camp in Debert, Nova Scotia, the following year. Realizing that Mum could no longer finance my career, I got jobs dancing in three short-lived musicals and spent a few months as lead dancer with the Mason Light Opera Company in Los Angeles. Then I answered a teaching ad from a Seattle newspaper and for the next two years headed the ballet department of the Constance Hart School in that city.

While teaching there, I received a letter from Norman Silk, by then a squadron leader with the RAF in Calcutta, telling me he had been hospitalized with rheumatoid arthritis but was recovering. Through our continued correspondence, a maturing and intimate relationship developed. When he was well enough to travel, Norman explained, the air force would ship him back to England where he would be honourably discharged from service.

Meanwhile, in Seattle I had successful auditions with both Alicia Markova and Anton Dolin of the American Ballet Theatre and was waiting for my contract when, on a visit to Vancouver, I auditioned for and was accepted into the Canadian Army Show (CAS). As a soldier with the show, I returned to England in 1943 and located Aunt Doffie in Exeter, where her cottage had become a haven for Canadian lads on leave. I telephoned Norman, who had been back in Britain for several months, and the following day he came to the army barracks in Aldershot bringing—to our first meeting in five years—the emerald he had bought for me in Calcutta. We became engaged right there in the sergeants' mess.

I hadn't been in Britain more than three months when a fall from a horse sent me to the Canadian Neurological Hospital in Basingstoke. Doffie promptly moved into a local bed and breakfast and made a heroic effort to visit me daily, as did Norman. She was jealous of him and constantly belittled him. Shortly after I returned to CAS staff as a newly commissioned lieutenant, Norman was diagnosed with a brain tumour. He died in December 1944. Doffie avoided ever speaking about him after his death.

In the next year and a half, I choreographed thirty unit shows and was responsible for the discipline and care of 90-odd women in CAS Overseas Division, earning the rank of captain along the way. After repatriation I married my ex-commanding officer, Rai Purdy, and we moved to New York where Rai became a TV producer with CBS. I took a stab at the Broadway dance scene but retired after a fall on the concrete stage at Radio City Music Hall. Rai's TV career thrived and I became a Westchester housewife. We had two children.

On a visit to Vancouver in 1956, I reconnected with Doffie who had returned there with a friend, Betty Cobbold. The two of them had a fling in real estate, redecorating and selling small properties, each time moving Granny Sweeny's delicate antique furnishings along to their next project. On this visit, though older and frailer, Doffie greeted me as a real pal. Over drinks in familiar crystal glasses, she treated me to her most sarcastic humour.

She and Betty moved back to Chelsea in 1960 where they lived in the poorest of flats. Doffie died in Betty's care, arthritic, bronchial and close to the end of her financial resources. Her possessions were willed to Betty for her lifetime; upon Betty's death, what was left of Granny Sweeny's furnishings were discovered in storage in Canada. They came to me because in the Sweeny family such possessions were handed down through the female side, and my late sister Moira and I were the only Sweeny women. They arrived in two Volkswagen crates—a bow-front Napoleonic consul table, sideboard, serving table, chests of drawers, mirrors, a marble-topped galleried roll-top desk with brass inserts, drop leaf desk, sewing table, dining table and chairs, and two beautiful little upholstered tub chairs with dolphins carved on their polished arms. After considerable work by Swift's Antiques of Vancouver, all except the tub chairs were restored to their former glory. The tub chairs, alas, were riddled with termites and had to be burned.

Granny's beautiful pieces of furniture, all of them well-proportioned and delicately detailed, have governed the interior design of each of the homes I have lived in since they came to me. And every time Doffie's portrait has taken its place of honour looking out over them from a new mantle piece, I know I am home. I did love her.